# THE BATTLE OF ALGIERS

GILLO PONTECORVO'S

# THE
# BATTLE OF
# ALGIERS

*A Film Written by*
## FRANCO SOLINAS

## PierNico Solinas
*Editor*

CHARLES SCRIBNER'S SONS / NEW YORK

1 3 5 7 9 11 13 15 17 19 C/C 20 18 16 14 12 10 8 6 4 2

Printed in the United States of America
Library of Congress Catalog Card Number 73-3915
ISBN 0-684-13433-0
ISBN 0-684-13437-3 (pbk)

*per mia madre*

Thank you:

Gillo and Picci Pontecorvo, Franco Solinas,
Ennio Morricone, Antonio Musu, Elisa and
Frank Michel III, Socrates Nicholas, Edward
J. Leiter, Pina Martello, Maristella Lorch,
Bruna and John Nelson, Louis Rossetto, Jr.
and—Annina.

# Contents

*Gillo Pontecorvo*

# Introduction

Deliverance through pain:
Gillo Pontecorvo's *The Battle of Algiers*

> What is your starting point? Either
> you believe in man or you don't.
> Both views are equally valid. My
> starting point: complete faith in
> man.
>
> ROBERTO ROSSELLINI

The fundamental misconception about *The Battle of Algiers*
concerns its "objectivity," which has been much acclaimed.
Actually the most stunning feature of the film is its ability to make
a subjective statement employing objective fact. For Gillo Pontecorvo the remaking of history, or shooting under what he calls
"the dictatorship of truth," is not simply a re-creation of past
events through *cinéma vérité* technique, nor the repiecing of history
for history's sake; it is, rather, a deliberate rearrangement of
chosen fact for a didactic purpose. Without adding fiction to the
facts he seeks to probe beneath the surface, by stripping history of
the superfluous and reducing it to its essentials, to re-examine and
re-evaluate the basic concept of the historical event in point. In
exploring its most significant implications, he seeks to draw from
history a critical conclusion that can exist independently of the
Algerian struggle. That very struggle becomes a proving ground
which Pontecorvo elevates to the level of an archetypal situation
from which a theory can be deduced. By illustrating the teachings
and methods of revolutionary struggle, *The Battle of Algiers* offers
a blueprint for other struggles and other revolutions. The Marxian
"union of theory and practice" is superseded by the more militant
"theory from practice." Thus the movie resists being dated or

limited to a specific historical setting. By transcending time, place, and characters it reaches out to condemn any so-called civilization that dominates, exploits, crushes people. The action takes place in Algiers but it could very well happen anywhere else; it could occur in any city with a ghetto where misery kills man, where colonialism—foreign or domestic—impedes him from living like a man.

With *The Battle of Algiers* Pontecorvo committed himself to redefining a reality which had been falsified and misrepresented. The nature of his commitment was bound to raise controversy as he attempts to shake an apathetic audience from its complacent existence by taking a stand unequivocally in favor of a people's struggle for self-determination. He refuses to offer a truth acceptable to all; he insists that his film divide the public, provoke it, force it to take a stand. Every component of his cinematic creation is geared toward the same purpose. The music does not merely accompany the action; at times it exerts the strength of visual image. It never distracts but is always functional. The dialogue, an ideological debate in dramatic form, serves to pinpoint the terms of the dialectic without frill or embellishment. Strictly linked to the rational sphere, it totally complements the image. The photography does more than realize the director's scope of total realism, it speaks a new cinematic language which reconciles the conflict between the exigencies of historical accuracy and the need for artistic creation. Pontecorvo sets rules of visual austerity and observes them throughout the movie. As a result the direction is always challenging, never slick. He avoids zany camera angles, editing gimmicks, or visual trickery for the solemn simplicity of a pan, the inherent dramatic impact of a close-up, the poignant understatement of a fade-out. In his determination to engage the audience and evoke from it a rational judgment, Pontecorvo begins his visual assault with the very opening sequences. The narrative is taken up *in medias res* with the shot of a freshly tortured Algerian supported by French paratroopers. This one shot, with its compelling sense of immediacy, has the total impact of a political statement. It is colonialism epitomized. This is the way Pontecorvo presents facts. Their meaning is clear and explicit; they embody ideas; they illustrate the political nature of ideas. Through his reconstruction, history loses its static quality of artificial chronology and becomes dynamic, vibrant, alive. It bursts into being as though it were happening for the first time. The gap of make-believe between viewer and screen is bridged.

The film deals with the revolutionary activity of a group of National Liberation Front partisans in the city of Algiers and its galvanizing effect on the people's growth to political awareness. Through guerrilla actions the NLF succeeds in raising the people from the stratum of *lumpenproletariat* to a powerful, tightly knit political force. This force then develops its own self-propelling impetus which will become the decisive factor in determining the outcome of the conflict. The real protagonists of *The Battle of Algiers*, then, are the people; and Pontecorvo has focused his narrative on them, tracing the process through which colonialism, once suffered individually, becomes a common foe. In Pontecorvo's hands the pain and privation of a people unjustly oppressed for so long is transformed into a severe modern tragedy whose most important "actors" are its most anonymous: a drunken derelict killed by small boys, a young candy seller lynched at the race track, an Arab street worker who becomes the victim of the growing paranoia sweeping the European city, a political prisoner hastily executed in the prison courtyard.

The film is without heroes. Even those characters sketched in greater relief are intentionally refused autonomy. They remain the director's instruments for expressing political positions. It is not important that they have a past or a future, a private life or a personal identification. Ali la Pointe, for example, typifies Ponte-corvo's conception of characterization in *The Battle of Algiers*. We first see him as an illiterate streetdweller living from day to day by his wits alone. He is playing three-card monte when a woman points him out to a policeman. Ali flees. We'll never know what he was accused of, nor does it matter. The incident is self-explanatory; it illustrates a typical episode in the relationship between coloni-zers and colonized. Pontecorvo crystallizes its significance by treating Ali's flight as reflex action. Only then does the narrator introduce him to us; and the introduction is simply a statement of his police record. The case history is Ali's, but could just as well belong to any product of the colonial system.

Pontecorvo chooses to have the people as sole protagonist to state that the struggle for national independence is a class struggle.

It is the confrontation of two opposing interests: the haves and the have-nots, with their respective concerns—the preservation or the revolutionary destruction of existing power relations. Ali la Pointe and Colonel Mathieu are their representatives. Alienated, crushed by an enslaving environment, actor of an existential adventure determined by others, Ali is seen as the product of a culture of poverty whose only status is desperation. Pontecorvo uses this beaten man to express how, as Frantz Fanon has rightfully pointed out, the rehabilitation of a people victimized by systematic and deliberate brutalization is possible only through violence; this is the sole means to counteract the effect of the violence they have had to endure. Colonel Mathieu, on the other hand, is portrayed as the personification of the inhumanity characteristic of bourgeois ideology. The role obliterates the individual; technology overshadows humanity. The subhuman end product of the bourgeois experience and the victim on whom subhumanity has been imposed—a victim only at the dawn of self-awareness—are worlds apart. In fact, Ali la Pointe and Colonel Mathieu never communicate. And it is with Ali's death that Pontecorvo emphasizes the total nature of class struggle. It is the ultimate statement. The ideological consistency of *The Battle of Algiers* is maintained to the very last scene. Instead of showing victory by giving way to a happy ending, it pits its opponents irreconcilably. Two societies are left in confrontation, one old and the other new, one static and the other coming of age. The film has recorded the crisis within the colonial system and warns that the struggle will be long, hard, and ruthless; it will be carried to total victory or no victory at all.

There is no doubt that with this film we are confronted with a major work. *The Battle of Algiers* is both an intensified reading of history and a testimony of incisive, poetic, and polemical impact. If on one level it teaches urban guerrilla warfare and attacks colonialism, on a deeper level it states a profound belief in man, in his craving for justice, his energy, and the purity of his ideals. It asserts that even the most abused people can reverse its relationship with history by acting upon events and molding circumstances. It is a film which cries out for action, not resignation.

Rome-New York                                    PierNico Solinas
Autumn 1972

# Credits *

| | |
|---|---|
| *Original Story by* | Gillo PONTECORVO and Franco SOLINAS |
| *Screenplay by* | Franco SOLINAS |
| *Directed by* | Gillo PONTECORVO |
| *Director 2nd unity* | Giuliano MONTALDO |
| *Director of Photography* | Marcello GATTI (A.I.C.) |
| *Art Director* | Sergio CANEVARI |
| *Music by* | Gillo PONTECORVO and Ennio MORRICONE |
| *Edited by* | Mario MORRA |
| *Assistant directors* | Fernando MORANDI (C.S.C.) and Moussa HADDAD |
| *Special effects by* | Aldo GASPARRI |
| *Produced by* | Antonio MUSU for Igor Film S.r.l.— Rome |
| *Production managers* | Sergio MEROLLE and Nour Eddine BHAHIMI |
| *Running Time* | 120 minutes |
| *Process* | Black and white |
| *Shot between* | July 25, 1966, and December 3, 1966 |
| *Length* | 3,280 meters |
| *Music Recorded* | R.C.A. Italiana and C.A.M. Spa. Rome |

* Credits as they appear in the print distributed in the U.S.A. The print also bears the following caption: NOT ONE FOOT OF NEWSREEL HAS BEEN USED IN THIS RE-ENACTMENT OF THE BATTLE OF ALGIERS.

*Processed by*            Istituto LUCE S.p.A.—Rome

*First shown*             In an uncut version at the Cinéma Afrique in Algiers in the presence of the government chief Haari BOUME-DIENNE, the members of the government, the Diplomatic Corp, Cardinal DUVAL.

*Presented in the U.S. by*   Gene WESSON, Albert SCHWARTZ, and Harry DIAMOND at "Cinema II" in New York City.

# Cast *

| | |
|---|---|
| COLONEL MATHIEU | Jean Martin |
| SAARI KADER | Yacef Saadi |
| ALI LA POINTE | Brahim Haggiag |
| HALIMA | Fawzia El-Kader |
| FATHIA | Samia Kerbash |
| PETIT OMAR | Mohamed Ben Kassen |
| THE CAPTAIN | Ugo Paletti |

* All non-professional actors except for Jean Martin.

# The Battle of Algiers
# Prizes and Awards

The Golden Lion at the 27th International Film Festival of Venice (1966)

The City of Venice Cinema Prize (1966)

The International Critics' Award (1966)

The City of Imola Prize (1966)

The Italian Silver Ribbon Prize: for best director
                                              best director of photography
                                              best producer

Ajace Prize of the Cinema d'Essai (1967)

The Italian Golden Asphodel (1966)

The Silver Goddess at the Acapulco Film Festival (1966)

The Golden Grolla (1966)

The Riccione Prize (1966)

Voted "Best film of 1967" by Cuban critics in a poll sponsored by Cuban magazine *Ciné*

Nominated in 1967 by the Academy of Motion Picture Arts and Sciences in the following categories:
    Best foreign language picture
    Best director
    Best original story and screenplay

The United Churches of America Prize for 1967

Screened by invitation at: Venice Film Festival 1966
                                          London Film Festival 1966
                                          Acapulco Film Festival 1966
                                          Moscow Film Festival 1967
                                          Edinburgh Film Festival 1967
                                          New York Film Festival 1967

# THE BATTLE OF ALGIERS *

Screenplay translated by
PierNico Solinas and
Linda Brunetto

---

\* A shooting script of the movie does not exist. Camera set-ups were determined as the filming progressed.

## VILLA HEADQUARTERS. INSIDE.
## NIGHT.

*Inside a three-story villa, just built, with whitewashed walls.
An elevator shaft is empty, the large cables dangle.*

*On every landing two apartments. The front doors are wide
open. Whitewash on the floor of the halls, swirls of whitewash
on the windowpanes, naked light bulbs hung from electric
wires. The rooms contain hardly any furnishings.*

*The kitchens are still without sinks and stoves.*

*An agitated bustle, a rhythm of efficiency. Paratroopers go
up and down the stairs, pass along the halls, enter and leave
the rooms.*

*The sounds in the background are indecipherable.*

SHOUTED ORDERS, CRIES, HOWLS.

SHOUTS, HALF-SPOKEN REMARKS, LAUGHS.

SOMEWHERE A GRAMOPHONE IS PLAYING AT FULL BLAST.

*The scene is tense. No pauses.*

*When the paras are tired, they move to another room.*

*They sit down, stretch out on the floor, drink coffee or beer,*

*and smoke cigarettes while awaiting the next shift. Suddenly,
the rhythm of this routine, the timing of these images is upset.
A* para *rushes down the stairs, and asks cheerfully while
running:*

MARC: The colonel. Where's the colonel?

PARAS: Why? What's happening?

MARC: We know where Ali la Pointe is. One of them "spoke" . . .

*His voice echoes through the corridors, on the landings, from
one floor to another. The excitement is contagious. Many
crowd around the door of the kitchen.
The Algerian who has "spoken" is there. He is young with a
thin face and feverish eyes. The* paras *are all around him:
they help him stand up, dry him, clean his face with a rag,
give him some coffee in a thermos cover. They are full of attention, sincerely concerned. One of them tries to push away
the others.*

PARA: C'mon, let him breathe!

*Meanwhile others who are arriving ask if it is true.*

OTHER PARAS: So he spoke? Does he really know where Ali is?

MARC: It seems so. We'll go see. Give him a little coffee.

*Marc is tall and husky, his eyes young and cheerful. One of
the others asks him with a shade of admiration:*

PARA: Hey Marc, you made him talk?

MARC (*smiling*): Sure.

*He then begins to smoke again, and moves aside to rest a bit.
The Algerian is trying to drink, but his hands are trembling.
Someone helps him and holds still the cover of the thermos,
drawing it to his mouth:*

LAGLOY: C'mon Sadek . . . Drink, you'll feel better.

*The Algerian drinks, but his stomach can't take it, causing
him to double over and vomit again.
Colonel Mathieu enters, elegant and graceful.*

MATHIEU (*smiling*): At ease. Is it true?

MARC: I think so. Rue des Abderames three . . .

*The colonel turns to the* para, *who had gone to call him, and who is holding a pair of camouflage fatigues in his hands.*

MATHIEU: Dress him.

*Then he goes near the Algerian, lifts his chin, inspects him for a moment with curiosity.*

MATHIEU: Chin up, it's all over. Nothing can happen to you now, you'll see. Can you stand up?

*The Algerian nods yes. The colonel turns to the* paras *who are holding him up.*

MATHIEU: Let him go.

*He takes the camouflage fatigues and hands them to the Algerian.*

MATHIEU: Here, put them on.

*The Algerian mechanically takes the fatigues, but he doesn't understand. The colonel explains to him:*

MATHIEU: We're trying to help you. We're going to the Casbah. Dressed like this, they won't be able to recognize you. Understand? We're going to see the place, then you'll be free . . . and under our protection . . .

*The Algerian shivers from the cold. He is completely naked. He laboriously puts on the fatigues which are too big for him.*

MATHIEU: Go on, give him the cap.

*They give him a wide belt and buckle it. The other* paras, *one on either side of him, roll up his sleeves to the elbows. A third places the cap on his head and cocks it.*

LAGLOY: Nationalized!

*The colonel turns to him angrily:*

MATHIEU: Don't be an idiot, Lagloy!

*The Algerian is ready. The* paras *look at him repressing their*

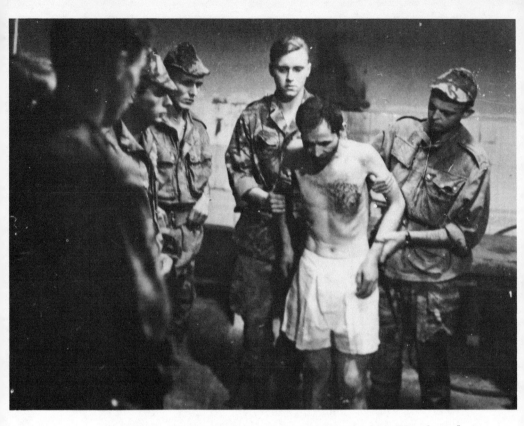

*laughter. The Algerian continues to tremble. His breath is short, his eyes glossy. He is crying.*

CAPTAIN: Let's go.

*The Algerian looks around. He breathes deeply. Then suddenly, unexpectedly, he lets out a hoarse cry:*

SADEK: No!

*and tries to jerk forward toward the window.*
*Marc seizes him immediately, and with his right hand grabs him by the chest, almost lifting him. With his left hand he gives him two quick slaps, not very hard.*

MARC (*persuadingly*): What do you think you're doing, you fool? Do you want us to start all over again? C'mon, be good. Don't make me look like an idiot in front of the others.

*He makes a reassuring sign to the colonel. Then he takes the
Algerian by the arms, and they move off.*

SCENE 2

STREETS OF ALGIERS. OUTSIDE.
DAWN. OCTOBER 7, 1957.

*The city is gray and white, by the sea which looks like milk.
The dawn outlines her features sharply.
The streets and wide avenues of the European quarters are
empty. Silence, until gradually is heard . . .*
A HUMMING OF MOTORS.
*One truck after another. Their headlights on, with an opaque
glow, by now useless.
A line of trucks follow one another along the sea-front, all
at the same speed.
They turn right and go up toward Place du Gouvernement.
Here, without stopping, the columns divide in two. The two
lines enter each of the two roads that lead up to surround the
Casbah.
In the brighter light, the Casbah appears completely white,
limestone. Enclosed by the European city, it stands at a
greater height and overlooks it.
Mosaic of terraces. White pavement, pavement interspersed
by the black outlays of narrow alleys. Only a jump from one
terrace to another . . .
Agile and silent, the* paras *jump one by one from the trucks
in a hurry.*
SOUND OF TRUCKS.
*They arrange themselves geometrically, their movements syn-
chronized. They disperse and disappear in the alleys.
They reappear together, then once again scatter.
They meet without looking at one another; each one takes his
own course.
In like manner without a sound, they are above, even on the
terraces, in perfect geometry. Even up here, the* paras *tighten
their grip . . .*

SCENE **3**

RUE DES ABDERAMES. COURTYARD
OF HOUSE. INSIDE/OUTSIDE. DAWN.

*Every three yards, there is a* para, *even at all four corners of
an intersection.*
*They are also in the side streets as well as the main streets.*
*And also above, against the sky, many other* paras *appear.*
*Number three. The doorway is the height of a man. A squad-
ron stands ready in a semicircle with machine guns in firing
position.*
*Marc continues to hold up the Algerian by his arm.*
*The captain glances at his watch, then looks up at the terrace
and gives a signal.*
*In a lowered voice, without turning around, he speaks to the
para who is at his back:*

CAPTAIN: Fire . . .

*The* para *nears the front door, his legs wide open, his machine
gun clenched at his side, and aims at the lock.*
MACHINE GUN FIRE.
*He moves the gunbarrel in a circular direction.*
*Immediately the others hurl themselves against the door.*
*At the same time, the door of the terrace is broken down, and
the* paras *burst into the house below.*
*The inner courtyard is square. In the center there is a well;
above, a patch of sky; on four sides, the arcades, columns, and
majolica arches. Beneath the porches, there is a door for every
dwelling. And above, a balcony with railings and other doors.
The doors are wide open. The* paras *quickly carry out their
orders.*
ORDERS, CURT AND BRIEF.
*The people are used to all this and know how to obey. The
scene takes place exactly as if it were an arranged maneuver,
a practice drill.*
*The rooms are emptied in a few seconds. The people are
crowded together in the courtyard.*
*Eyes wide with fright.*

*Men, women, and children with blankets and sheets thrown around their shoulders. By now, it is almost day. A soft light is diffused from above.*
*The Algerian walks with his head lowered, Marc on one side, the captain on the other.*
*They climb to the first floor and go along the balcony.*
*The Algerian stops in front of a door.*
*The captain murmurs softly:*

CAPTAIN: Here?

*The Algerian nods yes. They enter.*

SCENE 4

ALI'S ROOM. INSIDE. DAWN.

*The room is badly lit. There is a mattress on the floor, and another on the table, a cupboard against the wall, some chairs. Nothing else. At the back of the room to the left, there is a dividing curtain hung by a cord at medium height. The curtain is drawn and a large bed with brass headboards is visible. The Algerian points in that direction; the captain signals for him to go there.*
*They go forward silently, and push aside the curtain. There is a small light bulb hung on the wall beneath a small shelf covered with postcards and photos.*
*The baseboard all around is more than three feet tall and is covered by majolica tiles.*
*The Algerian points to a spot in the brick structure, on the back wall, between the headboard of the bed and a corner of the room.*
*Marc and the captain have their machine guns ready. The captain goes near the wall, his breath drawn, and begins to examine it.*
*He runs the fingernail of his thumb along the wall horizontally, between one row of tiles and another.*
*He taps the tiles at different places until he hears the plaster in the interstices crumble. He looks at the bit of plaster that is left in his nail.*
*He squeezes it in his fingertips; it is soft, newly laid.*

*Then he bends over, places his ear to the wall, and listens.
Suddenly he smiles.*

SCENE **5**

ALI'S HIDING PLACE. INSIDE.

*There isn't enough air in the hiding place. The four are forced
to breathe deeply. And in that small space their laborious
breaths resound like splashes.*

*Ali la Pointe has his eyes fixed upon the square patch of wall
that seals the hiding place. His eyes are large, black, slanted,
his eyelids heavy, somewhat lowered, so that the black of the
irises appears even blacker in the shadows, deeper and more
sullen.*

*Petit Omar is with him, a boy of twelve, and Mahmoud who
is eighteen. There is also Hassiba, a Kabyle girl, blond, blue-
eyed, and fair skinned.*

*The hiding place is only five feet high, and hardly holds
them. They are sitting or stretched out on the ground, close
to one another.*

*The entrance to the hiding place is blocked by the small patch
of wall which matches exactly the rest. It is held firm by
a bar through an iron ring attached at the center. On the other
side of the cell, above them, there is a hole for air.*

*They are tense and do not move. Their lips are dry, half-open,
and their breasts rise and fall in a difficult attempt to breathe.*

VOICE CAPTAIN (*off*): Ali la Pointe . . . the house is surrounded.
You haven't got a chance. Surrender. Let the child and the girl
come out, then you and the other one. Leave your weapons inside.
It's useless to try anything. Our machine guns are ready to fire—
you wouldn't have time. Do you understand?

*Ali's face is motionless and hasn't changed its expression.*

VOICE CAPTAIN (*off*): Ali, do you hear me? Listen! You are the
last one. The organization is finished. All your friends are dead
or in prison. Come out. You'll have a fair trial. Come out, surrender.

SOUND OF FOOTSTEPS, OTHER VOICES, CHEERFUL, INCOHERENT:
VOICES PARAS: Why are they breathing so heavily?
Fear . . .
Air . . . They haven't got enough air inside . . .

*And again the voice of the captain, clear and somewhat distant:*

CAPTAIN (*off*): Make up your mind, Ali? Do you want us to wall you in, or do you prefer that we blow you to pieces? . . . Alright. So much the worse for you.

*Ali's expression is still firm; his stare is dark and sullen.*

SCENE 6
VIEWS OF THE CASBAH. OUTSIDE.
DAY. NOVEMBER 1, 1954.

*The Casbah: compressed humanity, swarming in the alleyways, on the steps, in the cafes, in the Arab baths, in the mosques, and in the markets; a tangle of voices, gestures, faces, veiled women, eyes. Someone is putting up a handbill, another distributes them.*

SPEAKER: "National Liberation Front! Algerian brothers! The time has come to break loose at long last from the bonds of misery in which one hundred and thirty years of colonial oppression has kept us chained. The moment of struggle is near; our goal—national independence . . ."

SCENE 7
VIEWS OF THE EUROPEAN CITY.
OUTSIDE. DAY.

*The European city: reinforced concrete, asphalt, steel, lights, shop windows, buildings, automobiles. A steady rhythm of efficiency, music, cordiality, an apéritif.*

SPEAKER: "In order to avoid a fatal and bloody conflict, we propose an honorable program of discussion to the French authorities, on condition that they recognize the right of our people to self-government . . ."

*And the Algerians who work in the European city, the dockers, waiters, laborers, street-cleaners, farm-hands, and gardeners.*

SPEAKER: "Algerians unite! Be ready for action! The National Liberation Front calls you to struggle."

*Unemployed, peddlers, beggars, shoeshine boys . . .*

SCENE **8**

STREET CARD GAME. OUTSIDE. DAY.

*Two hands are moving; one over the other, they criss-cross with incredible speed; at the same time, they are shifting three small pieces of wood which appear to be identical. The hand movements are marked by a kind of Algerian . . .*
CHANT.
*From time to time, the pieces of wood are overturned for a split second so that the other sides are visible.*
*Robust hands, thick, unusually agile for their size.*
*The hands of Ali la Pointe, younger then, twenty-four years old.*
*A European quarter of Algiers, Coming and going of people, automobile traffic. On the sidewalk a small group of Europeans and two Algerian boys.*
*Other passersby stop to watch. The group crowds around the stand where Ali la Pointe is playing his game.*
*The entranced eyes of all present are staring at the pieces of wood.*
*Ali's hands seem to move by themselves.*
*His glance, always a bit sullen, apparently distracted, indifferent, passes from one face to another, and then to the street, from one side to another.*
*At fifty yards, a policeman. Two Europeans, a man and a woman, are speaking to him in an excited manner, and nudging him along pointing to Ali.*

WOMAN: Look! Yes, that's him!

*Ali is no longer singing. His hands have stopped moving.*
A POLICE SIREN IS HEARD.
*Ali pushes his way through the crowd.*
*He breaks into a run.*
*The policeman also begins to run.*

SCENE **9**

STREET. ALI'S FLIGHT.
OUTSIDE. DAY.

*The street is sloping. Ali flees, pursued by the policeman.*
*He dodges passersby with agility. He gains ground. But*
*nearby are heard . . .*
SIRENS
*and also in front of him.*
*Another two policemen; they too are running.*
*There is an intersection. At the corner, a cafe.*
GAY MUSIC.
*Young Europeans leaning against a shop window stop chatter-*
*ing and look.*
*Ali reaches the corner, crosses the street, passes by the bar.*
*There is a blond youth, about eighteen, who seems to be a*
*student who stretches out his foot, and pushes a chair in front*
*of him.*
*Ali stumbles and falls.*
*The youth attempts a laugh, and at the same time moves back-*
*ward.*
*Ali is lying face downward, but suddenly turns his head*
*toward the youth and stares at him. Then lifting himself by*
*his arms, he turns to look back.*
*The police are now twenty yards away.*
*Ali gets to his feet. For a split second, he hesitates. He hurls*
*himself against the youth, headfirst.*
*Using his head, Ali rams into the youth's face, striking him*
*in the nose and splurting blood everywhere.*

*The youth is unable to shout. He opens his mouth in the attempt, but the only result is a gurgling sound and blood. His friends intervene. Ali is surrounded. The police arrive. A mass of people jump on Ali, kicking him and striking him with their fists as long as they please. Finally the police aid Ali and disperse the crowd.*
*Ali is now in handcuffs and being led away.*
*More people have arrived. They are yelling, shouting insults, and spitting on Ali.*
*Ali passes in their midst protected by the police. He pays no heed to the fist blows, the shouts, the spits but seems neither to see nor hear, as if he were already resigned to having lost the battle this time, and were preparing to wait patiently for a better chance.*
*He is walking with an unfaltering step. His face is emotionless, oval, swarthy. His hair black and wavy, his forehead low and wide; his eyes large and slanted with eyelids somewhat lowered, his mouth firm and proud.*

SPEAKER: Omar Ali, known as "Ali la Pointe" born in Miliana, March 1, 1930.

EDUCATION: Illiterate.

OCCUPATION: Manual laborer, farm hand, boxer, presently unemployed.

FORMER CONVICTIONS: 1942—Oran Juvenile Court, one year of reformatory school for acts of vandalism.
1944—Two years of reformatory school for theft.
1949—Court of Algiers, eight months for compulsory prostitution and resisting arrest. Habitual offender.

SCENE 10

PARIS 1955. OUTSIDE. DAY.

*The air is clear and springlike. A 4 CV Citroen delivery van is parked in front of the Minister of the Interior warehouses. The rear door is open, the motor is running, a policeman is*

*at the wheel. Two workers in overalls exit from the ware-
houses.*

*Each one is carrying a box, and places it inside the van. The
boxes are made of seasoned wood, both of them rectangular.
They are each about eight inches long; one and two yards
high respectively. The two workers sit down inside the van,
toward the rear. They are facing toward the exterior. Their
feet are dangling and almost touch the ground.*

*The jolting movement of the van in motion causes them to
laugh.*

STREETS OF PARIS. *Spring. Girls with lightweight clinging
dresses. The two workers call them, whistle, gesture, and then
move off in the distance.*

ORLY AIRPORT. *The van stops in front of a warehouse. The
two workers jump to the ground, place the boxes on their
shoulders, and enter the warehouse.*

*The boxes are moving on a mobile ramp. There is a large
label on each one which says:* REPUBLIC OF FRANCE. MINISTER
OF THE INTERIOR. DESTINATION: BARBEROUSSE PRISON. AL-
GIERS.

# SCENE 11

ALGIERS. BARBEROUSSE PRISON.
OUTSIDE. MORNING.

*Barberousse prison is situated on the outskirts of the Upper
Casbah. It is an ancient fortress with thick, high surrounding
walls, which appear to vanish in contrast with the central
building which dominates them. The whole structure is
covered with limestone like the other houses of the Casbah.
Only the bars on the windows and the big gate are black.*

*The gate opens. A covered jeep enters the prison courtyard.
In the stronghold of the jeep are the two boxes sent from Paris.
Early morning. The sky is pale blue. In the prison courtyard,
the workers open the two chests and assemble the guillotine.
It is possible to see it from the cell windows that face the
courtyard. Faces of prisoners appear between the bars of
some windows.*

*The workers have disappeared. Only the delicate, makeshift structure of the guillotine is visible, its slender outline lengthened.*

SCENE 12

PRISON CELL. INSIDE. MORNING.

*In one of the cells there are about twenty prisoners. The cell is huge; there are two very high windows that almost reach the ceiling.*
*A prisoner is standing on the urine bucket, and looks outside through the barred window. On the ground there are some mats which serve as beds. Nothing else.*
*About ten prisoners are in a group, seated on the ground, and they are speaking in whispers.*
AD LIB DIALOGUE IN LOWERED VOICES.
*Two of them are playing with some stones on a chess-board drawn in the dirt; others are speaking among themselves. One is reading a Mickey Mouse comic book and laughing to himself. But all of them, in appearance and behavior, are distinguished from those who make up the more numerous group. These solitary men are different in some way, they are not ordinary delinquents.*
*Ali la Pointe is alone, withdrawn from the others, seated on the ground, his shoulders propped against the wall, his knees raised. He is barefoot. On his left ankle, directly above his foot, are tattooed two words in print: TAIS-TOI. His shirt is unbuttoned and on his chest are other tattoos in a strange design.*
*Ali looks at the group and seems to listen to their murmured words absent-mindedly. His expression is taciturn, reserved, and indifferent.*
*Ali turns to the prisoner at the window.*

PRISONER AT WINDOW: Look at them!

*Ali jumps to his feet. Everyone moves toward the two windows.*

*Ali moves away two yards at a quick pace, then runs toward the window, and grabbing hold of the bars, heaves himself up to it.*

*The condemned man turns and looks up toward the windows. He seems to smile although his face is motionless. In a soft voice, he speaks to those faces which appear behind the bars:*

CONDEMNED MAN: Tahia el Djez-air! *

*The political prisoners take up the phrase and recite it gutturally, keeping time to the steps of the condemned man.*

POLITICAL PRISONERS: Tahia el Djez-air!


SCENE **13**

PRISON COURTYARD. OUTSIDE.
MORNING.

*The condemned man walks toward the guillotine accompanied by guards and a priest reading the Koran. There is also the executioner wearing a black hood. The executioner tries to appear indifferent. The priest recites his prayers. The entire ceremony seems improvised and hasty. The epilogue is reached quickly.*
PRAYERS.
*The condemned man bends. The executioner places his neck in the right position, adjusts it, turns his head a bit, then pushes his body forward.*
*He releases the mechanism.*
*The blade falls, the head rolls. There is no longer a chorus. No one is chanting.*
*Ali's eyes have remained motionless.*
*Then from above, as the dismembered body is being carried away in a basket, as the priest, the guards, and the officer are leaving, as the workers dismantle the guillotine, from above, from the balconies of the Casbah, suddenly the "ju-jus" of the women are heard, dense likes the cries of birds, shrill, metallic, angry.*

WOMEN: Ju-ju . . .

* Long live Algeria!

SCENE 14

SMALL SQUARE. CASBAH. OUTSIDE.
DAY. JANUARY 1956.

*It is raining. The water runs along the gulleys of the narrow alleys. The white houses have turned spongy gray. The children of the Casbah are playing and spattering mud. Skinny and half-naked children with bloated bellies and hair cropped because of sores.*

*Their mothers call them in vain. They continue to run, play, and wallow in the mud with a despairing gaiety.*

CALLS. VOICES. SHOUTS.

*Petit Omar was then ten years old. He is slender, dressed in long pants and a jacket which is too large for him and torn so that he seems almost clownish. Calm and absorbed, he passes in the midst of the other children, but doesn't notice them or their games.*

*A small square on a sloping ascent.*

*In the center, a fountain. On the elevated side of the square, on a corner, there is a mosque.*

SOUNDS OF CHURCH MUSIC.

*Standing still at the foot of the steps is an Algerian in white cloak, and hood down to his eyes. Other people pass by. The Algerian is turned to one side so as not to be seen.*

*Petit Omar walks toward him and nears his back.*

*The Algerian turns; it is Ali la Pointe. He tells the boy with a tone of boredom and curtness:*

ALI: Go away!

PETIT OMAR: Men have two faces: one that laughs and one that cries . . .

*Ali looks at him incredulously and asks:*

ALI: And they sent you!

*The child slips a hand under his sweater to his chest.*

PETIT OMAR: Sure, something wrong with that?

*Omar takes out a piece of paper folded in four, and hands it to Ali.*

PETIT OMAR: Take it. Everything's written here.

*He turns away and begins to run.*

ALI: Wait!

*Omar stops running and turns to Ali.*

ALI: Come here . . . Come.

*Omar retraces his footsteps. Ali goes to meet him.*

ALI (*in a brusque manner*): Can you read?

PETIT OMAR: Sure . . .

*Ali hands back the paper.*

ALI: Read it.

PETIT OMAR: Here?

*Ali turns and looks around him. He squats on his heels in order to reach Omar's height.*

ALI: Here.

*It is still drizzling. Omar unfolds the paper and begins to read it.*

SCENE 15

RUE RANDOM. CAFE MEDJEBRI.
OUTSIDE/INSIDE. DAY.

*The following day at 5 p.m., rue Random. The street is fairly wide for a street in the Arab quarter and at this hour it is crowded with people. There are Algerians in traditional costumes and others in European clothes. Noisy and tumultuous background . . .*

VOICES, SOUNDS, WORDS—ALL MIXED TOGETHER.

*Veiled women with intent glances. Silent women who seem to float through the crowds, untouchable.*

*An Arab cafe filled with customers at the tables and bar. Through the large shop window, a smoky, steamy interior is visible. The cafe is located in rue Random, number 40.*

OMAR (*off*): There is an Arab cafe at rue Random 40. The owner's name is Medjebri. He is a police informer . . .

*Medjebri is standing behind the cash register, smiling, very busy. He is wearing a traditional costume. He is very clearly*

*visible through the shop window above the heads of the cus-*
*tomers.*
*In a doorway near the cafe there is a clock hanging from a*
*signboard in front of a store. It is five o'clock.*
*A French policeman enters the cafe.*

OMAR (*off*): Every day at 5 p.m., a French policeman goes to see
him. He stops for a few minutes to get information with the excuse
of drinking a cup of tea. You have to kill the policeman . . .

ALI (*off*): Not Medjebri?

*Medjebri moves away from the register, still standing behind*
*the bar, to where the policeman is seated. He greets him, and*
*hands him a cup of tea.*

OMAR (*off*): No. It says the policeman.

*The policeman is leaning on the bar. He is tall and husky,*
*and is wearing a scruffy uniform with a kepi pushed back*
*somewhat. Now his thick lips are sipping the scalding mint*
*tea.*

ALI (*off*): Okay . . .

*The large clock and store signboard. Standing in front, there*
*is a slender girl, veiled, her eyes darting in contrast with the*
*rigid form of her motionless body. Her arms are raised to*
*form an arch, her hands supporting the edges of a large basket*
*balanced on her head.*

OMAR (*off*): At the corner, right in front of the large clock, there
will be a girl carrying a basket. When the policeman comes out,
you will follow him together. At the right moment she will give
you a pistol. You have only to shoot . . . quickly and in the back.

*Now the policeman has finished drinking his tea. He makes a*
*sign to pay. Smiling, Medjebri refuses the money, and says*
*good-bye.*
*Ali approaches the girl. They exchange glances.*
*The girl puts down her basket which is filled with corn, and*
*rests it by her side.*
*She moves slowly toward the cafe. Ali walks beside her.*

*The policeman is coming out of the cafe. He rudely bumps into those who are entering.*

*He makes his way along the sidewalk, and moves further away, balancing his heavy body at every step.*

*Ali and the girl are about a yard away from him. They follow him, pushed along with the many others who are crowded on the sidewalk.*

*Then the girl plunges her hand into the corn. In a second, she places the revolver in Ali's right hand.*

*He holds it under his cloak. The policeman's back is a hand's-breath away. But Ali does not shoot.*

*He moves forward to pass by the policeman.*

*Alarmed, the girl looks at him, and tries to hold him back. She shakes her head as if to speak.*

*Ali smiles at her. His eyes have a hard glint.*

*He moves a few steps past the policeman. Suddenly Ali turns, lifts his arm as if to push his way through, and then stretches out his hand with the revolver aimed.*

*The policeman stops; his eyes are wide with fear. Instinctively he lifts his arms and opens his palms.*

*Terror paralyzes him.*

*Ali glances about him. Many people are moving away hastily, but others stand still in a circle and watch fascinated. Ali speaks to all of them, in a loud voice. His eyes are alight.*

ALI: Don't move! Look at him. You're not giving any orders now! Your hands are up, eh! Do you see him, brothers? Our masters aren't very special, are they?

*A sharp, metallic click. Ali tries a second time, presses the trigger again.*

SEVERAL CLICKS. REVOLVER EMPTY.

*Ali rolls the gun barrel; it is empty.*

*The policeman slowly lowers his hands. His right hand rushes to his holster.*

*Ali is ready to jump, throws away the gun, and starts to move forward.*

*He knocks down the policeman, who is overwhelmed, and falls backward.*

*The crowd moves away quickly. Ali starts to throw himself on the Frenchman lying on the ground, but stops halfway.*
*A thought restrains him. He turns and sees the girl who has picked up the revolver and hidden it again in her basket. Then she moves away hurriedly.*
*Ali curses angrily, then kicks the policeman's head twice, and runs after the girl.*
*He reaches her, grabs her shoulder so roughly that she shouts.*

ALI (*in a whisper*): Bastard! . . . Bitch!

*The girl struggles free from his grip. At the same time, they hear behind them . . .*
POLICE WHISTLES.
*The girl quickens her step.*

### SCENE 16
SIDE ALLEY WITH FRONT DOOR.
OUTSIDE/INSIDE. SUNSET.

*The girl arrives at a side street, enters it, and breaks into a run.*
*Ali is again beside her, but unexpectedly the girl enters a front door.*
*She bends, places the basket on the ground, removes the revolver, and hides it in her breast beneath her shawl. She gets up again and leaves the basket.*
*Ali blocks her way.*

ALI: Tell me what this joke is all about.

*The girl attempts to push past him toward the door.*

DJAMILA: Let's move now or they'll catch us.

*Ali grabs her by the arm, shakes her, and shouts uncontrollably:*

ALI: I want to know who sent me that letter. What's his name?

DJAMILA: He's waiting for you!

ALI: Where?

DJAMILA: We're going there . . . if you don't get us arrested first.

*The girl nods toward the street where two policemen are passing by hastily.*
*Ali moves backward into the shadow of the doorway. He regains control of his nerves, loosens his cloak, and lets it fall on the basket. He is dressed in European clothes, trousers and pullover.*

ALI (*pushing her ahead*): Move . . . go ahead. I'll follow you.

*The girl takes a look outside, then goes out.*
*Ali follows her a few steps behind.*
*By now it is dusk.*

SCENE 17
TERRACE. KADER'S HOUSE.
OUTSIDE. NIGHT.

*It is a starry night and there are few lights visible in the windows of the Casbah. In the background, there is the triumphant neon of the European city, the sea, the ships at anchor, the shining beams of a lighthouse. Kader turns around gracefully, and goes to sit on the wall of the terrace.*

KADER: You could have been a spy. We had to put you to the test.

*Ali looks at him sullenly.*

ALI: With an unloaded pistol?

KADER: I'll explain.

*Kader is a few years older than Ali, but not so tall. He is slender with a slight yet sturdy bone structure. The shape of his face is triangular, aristocratic, his lips thin, his eyes burning with hatred, but at the same time, cunning. He continues to speak in a calm tone which has an ironic touch to it.*

KADER: Let's suppose you were a spy. In prison, when the NLF contacts you, you pretend to support the revolution, and then the French help you to escape . . .

ALI: Sure. By shooting at me.

KADER: Even that could be a trick. You escape, then show up at the address which the brothers in prison gave to you, and so you are able to contact me . . .

ALI: I don't even know your name yet . . .

KADER: My name is Kader, Ali . . . Saari Kader . . . In other words, in order to join the organization, you had to undergo a test. I could have told you to murder the barman, but he's an Algerian . . . and the police would let you kill him, even though he is one of theirs. By obeying such an order, you still could have been a double agent. And that's why I told you to kill the French policeman: because the French wouldn't have let you do it. If you were with the police you wouldn't have done it.

*Ali has followed Kader's logic a bit laboriously, and he is fascinated by it. But not everything is clear yet.*

ALI: But I haven't shot him.

KADER (*smiling*): You weren't able to. But what's important is that you tried.

ALI: What's important for me is that you let me risk my life for nothing.

KADER: C'mon . . . you're exaggerating. The orders were to shoot him in the back.

ALI: I don't do that kind of thing.

KADER: Then don't complain.

ALI: You still haven't told me why you didn't let me kill him.

KADER: Because we aren't ready yet for the French. Before attacking, we must have safe places from which to depart and find refuge. Of course, there is the Casbah. But even the Casbah isn't safe yet. There are too many drunks, pushers, whores, addicts, spies . . . people who talk too much . . . people who are ready to sell themselves, undecided people. We must either convince them or eliminate them. We must think of ourselves first. We must clean out the Casbah first. Only then will we be able to deal with the French. Do you understand, Ali?

> *Ali doesn't answer.*
> *Kader has come down from the wall and looks toward the Casbah. Ali too looks toward the Casbah, immersed in the night.*

ALI: And how many are we?

KADER: Not enough.

# SCENE 18

AREAS OF CASBAH UNDERWORLD.
OUTSIDE/INSIDE. DAY.
MARCH 1956.

> *A warm spring wind, large white clouds. At the western edge of the Casbah, from the Upper to Lower Casbah, the street of the Algerian underworld descends to the brothel quarter.*

SPEAKER: "National Liberation Front, bulletin number 24. Brothers of the Casbah! The colonial administration is responsible not only for our people's great misery, but also for the degrading vices of many of our brothers who have forgotten their own dignity . . ."

> *Shady bars for gamblers and opium smokers, shops filled with tourist trinkets, merchants, fences, pimps, children with adult faces, ghastly old women, and young girls, whores standing in the doorways of their houses. The girls having their faces uncovered have put scarves on their heads, knotted at the nape.*

SPEAKER: "Corruption and brutality have always been the most dangerous weapons of colonialism. The National Liberation Front calls all the people to struggle for their own physical and moral redemption—indispensable conditions for the reconquest of independence. Therefore beginning today, the clandestine authority of the NLF prohibits the following activities:

> gambling

the sale and usage of all types of drugs
the sale and usage of alcoholic beverages
prostitution and its solicitation
Transgressors will be punished. Habitual trangressors will be punished by death."

SCENE 19

BAR. EUROPEAN CITY FACING
CASBAH. OUTSIDE/INSIDE. SUNSET.

*It is dusk. In the European city, the first lights are visible.
People begin to crowd the bars for an apéritif.
An Algerian shoeshine man leaves his workbox at the entrance
of the bar. He goes to the counter. He is tall and thin as a
reed. He takes from his pocket a handful of change; his hands
tremble slightly as he counts it.
The barman recognizes him, fills a glass of wine, and places
it in front of him. The Algerian pays and takes the glass. It's
probably not his first; the trembling of his hands increases.
The Algerian drinks the wine in one gulp, then goes to the
door. He waits patiently while some Europeans enter.
He goes out, picks up his workbox, and moves away.*

SCENE 20

RUE MARENGO AND STEPS. OUTSIDE.
SUNSET.

*The Algerian is standing at the top of some steep, almost
vertical steps that lead from the European quarters to the
Casbah.
Now he is in rue Marengo. There is still some daylight. The
street is crowded. The Algerian is unsteady on his legs. He
stops and mutters something to himself. It is obvious that he
is trying to hide his drunkenness.
He begins to walk, his hand against the wall for support. He
stumbles.*

*The workbox falls, scattering brushes and cans of shoe polish
on the ground. The Algerian bends down and begins to pick
up his tools. He is swearing.*
*Others have seen him. A peddler points him out to a child of
about ten. It is Petit Omar, who nods yes, then whistles.*
*Another whistle answers him, then another and another.*
*There are other children at every corner of the street.*
*They arrive in a run and gather together.*
*Omar points to the drunk who is now moving away, and gives
the order to attack. It is evident that this is not a game for
them, but a duty.*
*There is a chorus of brief shouting, of insults, and whistles.
The drunk sees them approaching. He is terrified.*
*He tries to quicken his step.*
*They reach him quickly and surround him. They attack him*

*and then flee, small yet elusive. They do not laugh even once;
their faces are hard and cruel.*
*The drunk swings around holding his workbox by its strap.*
*Some children are hit; some fall.*
*The drunk avails himself of this chance to escape, and re-
traces his steps to the staircase.*
*He begins to descend toward the European quarters. But the
children are again upon him.*
*They are shouting more loudly now, and pushing him. He
quickens his step, and staggering jumps the steps two by two.
The children trip him and he falls.*
*He is crying. He shields himself with his hands.*
*The workbox has fallen and is rolling down the steps. The
children are now on top of him, like small beasts on a carrion.
They smother him, push him and pull him. They are no
longer shouting.*
*All of them are intent upon their efforts. Only the drunk is
shouting despairingly.*
*They succeed in moving him, and hurl him down the steps.
He rolls downward, trying in vain to grab something with his
hands.*

SCENE 21

BAR CASBAH. OUTSIDE/INSIDE. DAY.

*Outside the sun's light is blinding. Inside the small bar there
is fresh air and shade.*
*A young Algerian, with lifeless eyes and an idle expression,
is rolling an opium cigarette. He lights it. Two slaps cause
the cigarette to fall from his lips.*
*Ali la Pointe is wearing a djellabah, a type of cloak without
buttoning which slips on over the head. There is an opening
of about eight inches at the waist.*
*Ali has stretched his arm through the opening to slap the
opium addict, who recognizes Ali, smiles, and makes a dazed
grimace.*

OPIUM-ADDICT: Ali la Pointe . . .

ALI: Wake up! Have you seen Hacene le Bonois?

OPIUM-ADDICT (*shaking his head*): Not today . . .

*Then he gets up laboriously, bends down, and looks for the cigarette that had fallen from his hand.*
*He doesn't reach it. Ali quickly crushes the cigarette with his foot. He is wearing a pair of sneakers. He moves away and leaves the bar.*

SCENE **22**

STREET BAR. CASBAH. OUTSIDE.
DAY.

*Ali continues to scour the streets. From time to time, without lingering, he asks someone:*

ALI: Seen Hacene le Bonois?

*Then adds:*

ALI: Tell him I'm looking for him . . .

SCENE 23

BROTHEL QUARTERS. OUTSIDE.
DAY.

OFF LIMITS

*Entrance to the brothel quarters. The street widens, the alleys branch off and seem to broaden. There are one or two Europeans, not only tourists in search of adventure, but also elements of the international criminal underworld who mingle here with the Algerians.*
*Almost all the buildings house a brothel or other place of ill-repute. On some doorways signs are hanging which read:*
THIS IS AN HONEST HOUSE.

SCENE 24

BROTHEL. INSIDE. DAY.

*Ali has entered a brothel. It is morning and there are few clients. The whores are Algerian and European. Some of them are pretty.*
*The madam is an Algerian, dressed in European clothes. She is about forty, heavily made up. When she spots Ali, she interrupts her usual professional chant. She seems curious, yet glad.*

MADAM (*shouting*): Ali la Pointe!

*She stops herself, already sorry for having spoken so quickly and imprudently. Ali doesn't answer her, but approaches with a steady and serious glance.*

MADAM (*changing tone*): Haven't seen you around for some time. I thought you were still in prison.

*Ali leans against the counter, never once taking his eyes off her.*

ALI: Is Hacene le Bonois here?

MADAM: No. He left early this morning. You know how it is with the boss . . .

ALI: I want to see him. If he shows up, tell him that I'm around.

*Ali moves away from the counter and turns. He leaves without a word. The woman tries to understand what has happened, and follows him with a worried glance.*

SCENE 25

SMALL STREET. HACENE. OUTSIDE. DAY.

HACENE: Ali, my son . . . Where have you been hiding?

*Ali turns suddenly, then pulls back so that his back is against the wall of the alley.*

ALI (*in sharp voice*): Don't move!

*Then he glances at the others.*

ALI: Hands still.

*The others are three young Algerians, Hacene's bodyguards. Hacene le Bonois is tall with short legs out of proportion with his enormous chest. He is somewhat corpulent. He has a wide face, a cheerful and self-confident expression. His clothing is a strange combination of Algerian and European which does not, however, appear ridiculous, but imposing. At Ali's remark, his expression changes, becomes amazed and baffled. But at the same time, his eyes give away the brain's attempt to find an explanation and a solution.*

HACENE (*astonished*): You know I never carry weapons . . .
    *Ali keeps his arms and hands hidden under his djellabah.*

ALI: I know.

*Hacene laughs warmly, and stretches out his hands which are enormous, thick and rough.*

HACENE: You afraid of these . . . ?

ALI: Don't move, Hacene.

HACENE: Why are you afraid? We've always been friends. One might even say that I brought you up . . . Isn't it true, Ali?

ALI: It's true.

HACENE: What's happened to you?

ALI: The NLF has condemned you to death.

*Hacene is stunned. He speaks aloud his thoughts in a soft voice.*

HACENE: Ah, so it's come to this . . .

*Then he bursts into loud laughter, and seems to turn to the three guards at his back.*

HACENE: I'm dying of laughter! Ha . . . ha . . . ha . . .

*Ali doesn't speak. He continues to stare at Hacene.*
*Hacene suddenly stops laughing. His tone of voice changes, becomes brusque and hurried.*

HACENE: How much are they paying you?

ALI: They're not paying me anything. They've already warned you twice; this is the last warning. Decide.

HACENE: What . . . What must I decide?

ALI: You've got to change occupations, Hacene. Right away!

*Hacene makes a gesture as if to emphasize what he is going to say.*

HACENE (*with irony*): Okay, you convince me.

*Then suddenly, unexpectedly, he lets out a . . .*
SHRILL SCREAM,
*like fencers who before plunging their swords, try to frighten their adversaries.*

*Simultaneously, he hurls himself forward, head lowered and arms outstretched.*
*Ali steps aside, and releases a*
BLAST OF MACHINE-GUN FIRE.
*Hacene falls flat on his face. There is movement. Some passersby approach. The three boys try to escape.*

ALI *(shouting)*: Stop!

*The barrel of the machine gun is visible through the opening in his djellabah. Ali's voice is quivering angrily:*

ALI: Look at him well! Now nobody can do whatever he wants in the Casbah. Not even Hacene . . . least of all you three pieces of shit! Go away now . . . go away and spread the word . . . Go on!

SCENE **26**

WEDDING. OUTSIDE. DAY.

*Summer. There is a garland of flowers strung across an alley.*
*A front door is open, and the guests continue to arrive.*

SCENE **27**

WEDDING HOUSE. OUTSIDE. DAY.

*In the inner courtyard, there are benches and chairs arranged*
*in rows. In front of all of them, there are two chairs separated*
*from the rest, one next to the other. In front of them, there*
*is a small table with a pen and inkstand on top. The people*
*remain standing, about twenty Algerians, of all ages. They*
*are speaking among themselves in thick whispers. There is an*
*expectant and ceremonious atmosphere.*

BUZZING.

*Mahmoud was seventeen then. He has soft down on his cheeks,*
*his first beard. He is thin, his neck long and terse, his glance*
*nervous. He appears to be the protagonist of what is about to*
*take place. His hair is combed with care and covered with*
*much hair cream. He is wearing a clean and newly bought*
*white costume.*

*Many of the others come to speak with him; the younger ones*
*are joking and trying to provoke him.*

AD LIB REMARKS.

*Mahmoud reacts comically with a grim frown with which he*
*tries in vain to hide his shyness. At the same time, he glances*
*secretly, anxiously, up to the empty balcony on the first floor.*
*Much gay and lively chattering can be heard from an open*
*door above.*

## SCENE 28

WEDDING ROOM. INSIDE. DAY.

*In the room, a group of girls are busy preparing trays with cups of coffee. They are little more than children, twelve or thirteen years old, with soft complexions, white teeth, and shining eyes. They seem children who are playing, but beneath that veneer of gaiety, some anxiety is noticeable, emotions in suspense. The faltering voice of an old woman calls from the adjoining room.*
*A girl leaves the group, lifts the dividing curtain, and nearing the bed where the old woman is lying, she kneels beside her. The old woman lifts her hand and places it on the girl's hair, caressing her tenderly. She speaks in a wavering voice, and her small yet kind eyes fill with tears.*
OLD WOMAN'S SPEECH IN ARABIC.
*The girls nods yes, then she gets up and goes to rejoin her companions. Passing before a mirror, she stops a minute to tidy her hair.*

## SCENE 29

HOUSE WEDDING. OUTSIDE. DAY.

*They appear on the balcony, then descend to the courtyard.*
*The nervous glance of Mahmoud scans their faces, then rests upon that girl who, with lowered eyelids, also glances quickly at him. Meanwhile the trays are being passed among the guests.*
*Now the people turn to face the front door. A young man has entered carrying a briefcase under his arm. Behind him are two boys who seem to be his bodyguards, and are the only ones dressed in European clothes. Both of them have their right hands under their jackets, which are old and torn. They seem to be armed. They close the door, and remain standing on either side of it.*
*The man with the briefcase walks toward the table. All pres-*

ent look at him respectfully. He smiles, responds to their greetings, shakes hands with all. But he refuses coffee and seems to be in a hurry.

He sits down, places his briefcase on the table, opens it, and takes out a large notebook. From the open briefcase, the metallic butt of a sub-machine gun appears.

On the cover of the notebook is written: NLF—ALGERIAN AUTONOMOUS ZONE. CIVIL RECORDS.

He turns the pages of the notebook until he reaches the last written page. Then he glances up toward the people who, in the meantime, have taken their seats. He smiles, says a few words, then calls two names.

Mahmoud walks forward stiffly, erect, his eyes staring straight ahead of him.

The girl also walks forward, with a perplexed expression. They sit down next to each other, but without looking at each other. The ceremony consists of a few words. Finally the two youths look at each other. Mahmoud tries to smile, but he cannot.

The girl's expression softens somewhat. Her glance is tender; she lowers her face quickly. Meanwhile the others recite the verses of the Koran in low voices.

CHORUS.

## SCENE 30

RUE D'ISLY. OUTSIDE. DAY.
JUNE 20, 1956. 8:05 A.M.

There is a French guard, no more than thirty years old. He has a blond mustache, his beard recently shaven. There are few people in the street. The guard walks slowly, glancing in the shop windows from time to time to admire his reflection. He stops, adjusts his cap, and smiles.

An Algerian appears beside him; he is also young. The guard pretends to be interested in the photographic equipment which is on display, then moves on.

The Algerian's arm springs forward and returns quickly to its place. He plunges the knife into the guard's neck.

*The guard opens his mouth wide to shout, but he cannot.
The blood gurgles in his gashed throat. None of the few
passersby has seen what happened. The guard falls flat on
his face. Someone sees him and screams.*

*The Algerian hurls himself on top on the soldier, opens his
holster, takes his pistol, then gets up pulling the gun with him.
The gun is fastened by a leather cord. The cord gets tangled
in the gashed neck of the guard.*

*The Algerian pulls in vain. He panics. He looks about him
with terrified eyes.*

*People approach hurriedly. They are shouting. The Algerian
pulls the cord a second time, desperately.*

*He regains his control, picks up the knife which is lying on
the ground, and cuts the leather cord, thus freeing the pistol.
The others have almost reached him and he is surrounded, but
he manages to dodge them, and escapes.*

SCENE 31

BOULEVARD BRU. OUTSIDE. DAY.
8:40 A.M.

*A group of zouaves on patrol, three soldiers and an officer.
The street is sloping; on the right there is a high fence covered
with advertising signs and cinematographic posters, all of
them torn and full of holes; the emptiness on the other side
is visible through the holes.*

*The soldiers are chatting among themselves and looking at
the posters.*

*A soldier stops because he sees something moving on the other
side of the fence.*

*He points to it and shouts, but not in time.*

MACHINE-GUN FIRE INTERRUPTED BY SINGLE SHOTS.

*The soldier falls, the others remain motionless, unbelieving.
They begin to run and scatter and look for cover.*

*An Algerian appears on top of the fence. He moves like a cat,
and jumps from the other side.*

*His invisible companions continue to shoot. He is unarmed,
and runs to the dead soldier. He grabs the machine gun and*

*retraces his steps. The action takes place in a second.*
*By now the soldiers too are shooting, but it is too late.*

SCENE **32**

POLICE STATION. CHEMIN AIN-
ZEBOUDJA. OUTSIDE/INSIDE. DAY.
9:10 A.M.

> *A police station in the Casbah, a small prefabricated one-story*
> *building.*
> *At the main door there is a police guard. A group of five Al-*
> *gerians is approaching. They are talking among themselves,*
> *and gesticulating.*
> BUZZING.

*The policeman enjoys watching them, then asks what it's
about. All five of them answer him at once, trying to outdo
one another.*
*The policeman has to shout to make them keep quiet.*
*Then, assuming a very humble behavior, they enter silently.
The oldest among them speaks in a mournful voice. He seems
to be crying and asks the sergeant something.*
*The policeman calls a colleague, and tells him to accompany
the Algerians. Four of them go with the policeman, while
another remains in the waiting room, saying that it is better
because he is afraid of losing his control.*
*Then he begins to explain the reasons for the quarrel: it con-
cerns a will. The old man is his grandfather, but he has recently remarried. Then from inside is heard . . .*
MACHINE-GUN FIRE.
*The policeman reacts quickly and tries to draw his gun. But
the Algerian is faster and fires point-blank.*
*The four reappear. One of them is wounded. All of them are
armed with revolvers, and carry at their sides a machine gun
and two sub-machine guns that they have taken from the
armory. Other cries and shots are heard behind them.*
*All five of them run out in haste.*

SCENE **33**

RUE MARENGO. OUTSIDE. DAY.
9:45 A.M.

*Another police station. Two policemen are chatting in front
of the entrance.*
*A black Renault is passing by at a walking speed, then slows
down almost to the point of halting completely.*
*The right door opens and there is a burst of machine-gun fire.
One of the policemen has been hit, and grabs the other so as
not to fall.*
*Another burst of . . .*
MACHINE-GUN FIRE.
*The two policemen fall down together. The car motor is ac-
celerated, the tires screech and the Renault shoots forward.*

*A military jeep arrives from the opposite direction, crashes
into the car and blocks its escape.*
*An Algerian flees and is pursued. Another descends from the
auto with his hands raised.*
*The soldiers shoot and kill him.*

SCENE**34**

AVENUE DU 8 NOVEMBRE. OUTSIDE.
DAY. 1:10 P.M.

*A large garage with workshop and filling station. In front are
some automobiles and a military truck.*
*A scooter with two Algerian boys passes by, rumbling noisily
along the road. Then at full speed, it makes a sharp turn, retraces its steps and turns again. The boys seem to be showing
off for fun.*
*Meanwhile, the employees of the garage are leaving their
work since it is lunchtime. The attendant at the gasoline
pumps is left alone.*
*The scooter stops in front of the high-test gasoline pump. The
attendant is a European, an elderly man, who approaches
them holding in one hand some bread he has just unwrapped.
He detaches the pump handle of high-test, and asks how many
gallons.*
*One of the Algerians points a revolver at the attendant, and
tells him to pour out the gasoline on the ground all around.
The other, meanwhile, goes to the other two gasoline pumps,
detaches the handles, and fastens them in an open position
in order to empty them of gasoline. He uses two pieces of
iron that he has brought with him to clamp the handles open.
He stretches the pump hoses as far as they can go toward the
garage and the parked cars.*
*The gasoline flows all over the large square. The two youths
are again on the scooter; they tell the European to move away.
They have soaked a rag in gasoline and they light it.*
*The gasoline continues to flow from the two open pumps. The
European is by now far away, the scooter is already moving*

*away, and at the same time, the boys hurl the lit rag into the square. It immediately bursts into flames.*

SCENE 35
COMMISSIONER'S OFFICE. INSIDE.
NIGHT.

*The night of the same day, in an office of the police commissioner's headquarters. On the desk, photos of the day's terroristic attempts are piled in a heap. An employee is in front of his typewriter.*
*The Assistant Commissioner is about forty years old, very robust. His face is somewhat wide, ordinary, and with heavy features. He leafs through the photos while speaking on the telephone. It is a very warm night, and the window of the office is open. From outside is heard the . . .*
SOUND OF TRAFFIC.

ASSISTANT COMMISSIONER (*on telephone*): Yes, sir, but they haven't received a search-warrant yet. Rue d'Isly? We followed them for a while, but then we lost track . . . Yes, sir, but it is in another precinct. No, it wasn't in theirs . . . There are some suspects for rue Marengo . . . No . . . the judge hasn't given permission yet. He is requesting a formal investigation first. Yes, sir, yes . . . Yes, sir, yes—But we haven't enough men. Of course, I understand . . . If it were possible, sir, you should . . . but the Commissioner can't . . . in . . . But couldn't you . . . Alright, sir . . . We'll let them cut our throats then!

*He slams the receiver angrily and begins to dictate his report. His voice is harsh, filled with rancor.*

ASSISTANT COMMISSIONER: TIME: 3 P.M. Attempt at homicide against a Patrol of the 3rd B.P.C.

PLACE: Luciani street at El Biar.
WEAPON: Revolver 7.75.
VICTIM: A soldier wounded in the right leg and groin. Hospitalized.
ASSAILANTS: Unknown.

TIME: 3:35 P.M. Homicide.

PLACE: Chopin Street, opposite number 20.

WEAPON: P.M. 38.

VICTIM: Private second-class Dare Jackie, born March 12, 1931. Deceased.

ASSAILANT: A moslem. Height: five feet and seven/eights inches. Light colored clothing. Probably escaped in Simca. License plates unknown.

TIME: Four minutes past 4 P.M.
Homicide and attempt at homicide against patrol of border guards.

PLACE: Intersection between Consular Street and General Laquiere . . .

Wait a minute . . .

*The officer stops speaking, takes a glass from his desk, and goes near the window. On the ledge, there is a bottle of beer, left there evidently to keep it a bit cool. He takes it, fills his glass and drinks.*
*Then he speaks in a lowered voice, while looking outside, without even giving any directions to the employee who waits with his hands poised about the keyboard of his typewriter.*

ASSISTANT COMMISSIONER: I want to see the newspapers tomorrow. If they're still talking about *pacification* of our *Moslem brothers!*

*He returns to his desk.*

ASSISTANT COMMISSIONER: Where were we?

EMPLOYEE: Intersection, between Consular Street and General Laquiere Avenue . . .

SCENE 36

VARIED FLASHES. POLICE STATIONS.
OUTSIDE. DAY.

*In front of police stations: Ain-Zeboudja . . . rue Marengo . . . and all the others . . . in the Casbah . . . in the European quarters . . . sandbag entrenchments are being pre-*

*pared, barbed wire is being stretched, metallic lookout turrets are being set up. It is very hot. Workers and policemen work in silence. There is an oppressive atmosphere.*

SPEAKER: "Ordinance of the Prefecture of Algiers: All police stations in Algiers, without exception and until further notice, are required to prepare and maintain external protection devices. The shifting of guards outside must continue uninterrupted twenty-four hours a day. Sentinels must be equipped with automatic weapons . . ."

SCENE 37

EUROPEAN AND CASBAH
PHARMACIES. MUSTAPHA HOSPITAL.
OUTSIDE/INSIDE. DAY.

*View of pharmacies in the European quarters and in the Casbah.*
*The shelves, medicines; people who are buying. The Mustapha hospital, reserved for Algerians. The wards: hospitalized Algerians.*

SPEAKER: "The Governor-General of Algiers decrees:
Article No. 1—The sale of medicinal and pharmaceutical products, effective for the cures of gunshot wounds, can be made only to those who present written authorization from the Commissioner of Police.
Article No. 2—Directors of all hospitals and clinics must produce to the police authorities an immediate listing of all patients admitted to their institutions for the care and treatment of gunshot wounds."

SCENE 38

CASBAH ROAD BLOCKS. OUTSIDE.
DAY.

*The Casbah is being closed off. Every point of entrance, every alley, every street that joins the Casbah and the European*

*quarters has been blocked off with wooden horses and with barbed wire nine feet high.*
*There are also workers, policemen, and soldiers who are working at the barricades.*
*Beyond them, on the other side of the barbed wire, the Algerians seem to be encaged.*

SPEAKER: "The Prefecture of Algiers states: In the course of these last few days, dozens of assaults have been committed in this city. We have reason to believe that the assailants originate in the Casbah, and that they have always found a speedy and easy refuge in the alleys of the Arab quarters. As a result, and in order to alleviate without delay the insecurity that now reigns in the city, the Prefecture of Algiers has decided that entrance to the Casbah can only be permitted at those points in the blockade under military control, where citizens in transit must exhibit their documents at request, and submit to eventual searches."

*The Casbah is imprisoned, like a huge concentration camp. Only five streets have been left open, the widest streets. There are five exits where the wooden horses serve to restrict passage, and where some wooden posts for the guards are being built.*
*Every exit is marked by a sign with large lettering.*

SCENE 39

BLOCKADE MARENGO. OUTSIDE.
DAY. AUGUST 10, 1956.

*At each blockade, there are two ramps, an entrance and an exit to the Casbah. The Algerians and some Europeans crowd around in both directions. The soldiers are wearing fatigues with helmets and machine guns. The Europeans are not requested to show identity papers.*
*The Algerians are often frisked, and accept this fact silently, patiently, without any sign of intolerance. But if the soldiers attempt to search a woman, then it is different.*
*A woman begins to shout, while waving her arms wildly, and*

*pushes away the soldier who had tried to search her. A stream
of incoherent words.*
*Other Algerians intervene; they push forward threateningly.
The soldier is young; he is timid and frightened. He looks
over his back for help.*
*A police officer approaches. He has a different tone, and a
very self-assured manner. He shouts at the Algerians to calm
down.*

OFFICER: Are you mad, touching one of their women? Go on, go
on, alright . . . Go ahead, keep moving!

*The woman passes the blockade, but still continues her protest
with a shrill and unbearable voice.*

SCENE 40

RUE PHILIPPE. OUTSIDE. DAY.
8:35 A.M.

*An Algerian woman walks along the sidewalk. She is elderly,
fat, and is wearing a traditional costume with her face veiled.
She walks slowly toward a bar, which has its tables outside,
and already some customers.*
*Near the bar, leaning against a wall, there is an Algerian who
now begins to move and goes to meet the old woman. They
greet one another with much warmth, like a mother and son
who haven't seen each other for a long time.*
*They embrace, and the man searches at her breast among the
folds of her veil. He finds a revolver which is hung by a cord,
and grabs it. They are at ten or twelve feet distance from the
bar. At a table, there is a French soldier having coffee with
cream, croissant, and an open newspaper.*
*The Algerian continues to embrace the old woman, and aims
from above her shoulders. Only one shot; the newspaper rips,
the soldier tries to get up again, his face full of blood. Then
he collapses on the table.*
*The Algerian has hidden the revolver in the woman's veil.
The two separate from their embrace. They seem terrified
and surprised, and move away from each other in different*

directions while the people are rushing about and . . .
SHOUTING.

SCENE 41

DE LA LYRE MARKET. OUTSIDE.
DAY. 9:10 A.M.

*The cries of the peddlers are loud and incoherent. An Al-*
*gerian is squatting on his heels, in front of his wares scattered*
*on the ground: clusters of aromatic herbs, jars of spices. A*
*youth is in front of him, and from time to time, he looks*
*around him. He seems to be waiting.*
*Now he bends down and begins to rummage through the*
*herbs. He selects a bunch of mint, weighs it in his hand, and*
*argues the price with the peddler.*
*A policeman in the market passes nearby and watches.*
*The youth waits a second, then turns toward the back of the*
*policeman, and stretches out his arm.*
*He has in his hand the bunch of mint; a revolver is hidden*
*among the greens. He shoots twice.*
*The French policeman falls down. The youth drops the mint*
*with the revolver among the other herbs, and moves away in*
*the midst of the crowd.*

SCENE 42

RUE DE BAR-EL-QUED. OUTSIDE.
DAY. 10:15 A.M.

*In front of the police station there are sandbags and a police*
*guard at duty with helmet and machine gun. The policeman*
*jumps to attention and salutes. An officer has come out of the*
*station and returns his salute. He moves away and walks*
*along the sidewalk.*
*There are few people. An Algerian seems to appear from*

*nowhere, and walks behind him. He is very young, is wearing
a short-sleeved shirt and blue jeans.
The officer turns at the first corner. Further on, there is a row
of cars and a metallic sign which warns that the parking space
is reserved for police vehicles only.
The officer hears the steps of the boy behind him, and summons him in a brusque manner.*

OFFICER: What are you doing here? Where are you going?

*The boy shrugs his thin shoulders and lowers his head.*

BOY (*in servile tone*): I'm going for a swim; my friends are waiting for me.

*The officer curses under his breath and proceeds. He stops in
front of a Dyna-Panhard, parked not too far away.
The boy moves on a few yards past the automobile until he
reaches a metallic wastebasket which is fastened to the pole
of a street lamp. He stops there, then glances around.
The officer is not far behind him; he has taken his car keys
from his pocket, and is about to open the car door.
The boy plunges his hand into the basket, rummages among
the torn papers, then suddenly turns, points a revolver·at the
officer's back, and shoots.
The man tries to clutch something, but slips and falls down.
The boy shoots again at the man on the ground, then plunges
his hand again into the wastebasket, drops the revolver, and
glances around him. He breaks into a run.
The policemen come out of the police station hurriedly.
Whistles, orders, excited cries.
They turn the corner. Some rush to the man lying on the
ground. Others jump into a jeep. Four of them jump on
motorcycles that are lined up in the rack. They move off in
two directions.
At the same time, wails of police sirens moving nearer are
heard in the distance. The street is deserted. There is no trace
of the boy. People are seen at their windows.
The officer is lifted by his arms.
An ambulance arrives and stops, its siren at full blast, its
doors wide open. The officer is placed inside.*

*The motorcycles are racing through the sidestreets. The jeep converges on them, then reverses its direction, moving while balanced on two wheels.*
*Passersby stop to watch, all of them Europeans. The siren's wail is at a high pitch.*

SCENE 43

ADJACENT STREETS. OUTSIDE. DAY.

*A deserted street, recently covered with wet asphalt.*
*A Moslem road worker is sitting on the ground next to a steam-roller. He is eating his lunch. The combined sounds of the siren's wail and the rumbling of the motorcycles are heard approaching.*
*Two motorcyclists appear in the street, passing by the road worker.*
*One of them stops and turns around.*
*The road worker moves backward to the street corner. He breaks into a run. His eyes are burning with fear, his face is anxious, undecided.*
*From the windows, the people point to him, and shout after him.*
*A jeep appears in the street in front of him.*
*The motorcyclist approaches from the opposite direction.*
*The Algerian stops running; he doesn't know what to do.*
*From the windows, continuous*
SHOUTING.
*The Algerian leans against the wall, watches the scene, and begins to cry. The policemen jump down from the jeep and leap at him. The Algerian isn't able to speak, but only shakes his head.*

SCENE 44

POLICE STATION. INSIDE. DAY.

*A room inside the police station. The Algerian's face is beaten from right and left by a series of slaps.*

*The room is filled with policemen. All of them are practically on top of the Algerian; all of them are shouting. In the confusion can be heard . . .*
SHOUTS.

VARIED VOICES: Do you know he's dead, you bastard? Do you know you killed him?

*They try to reach him, pushing against one another in order to get closer and hit him. The Algerian is crying and speaks in broken-off phrases, half Arabic and half French. His continual efforts to repeat certain words are heard:*

ALGERIAN: No, no, no, no, . . . me no . . . Viva France . . .

*An officer arrives making his way.*

OFFICER: Get out, go on, outside . . . Get out of the way! Go away . . .

*They make way for him; he reaches the Algerian who tries to smile at him, continually shaking his head:*

ALGERIAN: Sir . . . sir . . . sir . . .

OFFICER: What's your name?

*The Algerian's mouth is dry; he tries to swallow.*

ALGERIAN: Sir . . . sir . . . sir . . .

OFFICER: What's your name?

ALGERIAN (*straining, still trying to swallow*): Lardjane Boualem, sir . . .


SCENE 45

COMMISSIONER'S OFFICE. INSIDE.
NIGHT.

*In the Commissioner's office, the Assistant Commissioner dictates:*

ASSISTANT COMMISSIONER: Guilty: Lardjane Boualem, manual

worker, married with three children. Resident in rue de Thèbes, number eight . . . So? How many today?

*The employee removes the copies from the typewriter and begins to put them in order.*

EMPLOYEE: Seven assaults, three dead.

*Then he moves to the desk, and hands over the various copies for signature.*

EMPLOYEE: Here, one for the Commissioner . . . the press offices . . . the archives . . . and one for you, sir.

*The Assistant Commissioner signs.*

ASSISTANT COMMISSIONER: Good, thank you, Corbiere. . . . See you tomorrow.

EMPLOYEE: Good evening, sir.

*The employee salutes, then moves toward the door. He is about to go out when the Assistant Commissioner stops him.*

ASSISTANT COMMISSIONER: Tell me . . . Where is this rue de Thèbes?

EMPLOYEE: Rue de Thèbes? In the Upper Casbah, I think . . .

ASSISTANT COMMISSIONER: All right. See you tomorrow, Corbiere.

EMPLOYEE: Good evening, sir.

*The employee leaves and closes the door. The Assistant Commissioner crosses the room to the large map of Algiers which covers the entire wall. He moves his finger along the Casbah zone; as he moves it, he follows it with his glance in that tangle of streets.*

ASSISTANT COMMISSIONER (*to himself*): Rue de Thèbes . . . de Thèbes . . .

*He has found it. He observes it for a minute, then moves his finger along the road leading to the European quarters. He finds the right route, then concentrates in order to memorize it.*
*He returns to the desk, lifts the receiver, and dials a number.*

ASSISTANT COMMISSIONER (*on the phone*): Hello, Engineer Henry Arnaud, please . . . He's already left? Alright, yes, yes, alright . . . I have the number.

*He clicks the receiver, then dials another number. At the other end of the line, a feminine voice is heard. The Assistant Commissioner abandons his usual peremptory tone.*

ASSISTANT COMMISSIONER: Hello, Bernardette . . . Yes, right away. I'm going to change my clothes first, and I'll be right there. My wife is already there, right? No, it's not important. But call Henry for me. Just for a minute . . . Alright . . . thanks . . .

*He places the receiver on the desk, then puts on his jacket which is on the back of his chair. He straightens his tie.*
*Now from the receiver a muffled voice is heard; the Assistant Commissioner picks up the receiver.*

ASSISTANT COMMISSIONER: Hello, Henry? . . . Everything's okay. Good. What are we going to tell our wives? . . . The club? Good idea, yes. I'll be there right away. Just give me time to change my clothes . . . Ah, I've found the address. No, it's better to talk in person. Yes, it's the right place . . . Okay. Bye.

*He puts down the receiver, then goes to the coat-hanger and takes his beret. He goes out after glancing again at the photos of the day's assaults.*

SCENE 46

HENRY ARNAUD'S HOME. INSIDE.
NIGHT.

*Two small children are kneeling in front of their beds.*

CHILDREN: Notre Père, dans le ciel . . .

*Two children, five or six years old, blond, charming, but not affected. They seem to be twins, and are wearing identical pajamas.*
*At the same time, a servant is preparing their beds for the night. She is about fifty years old, her apron clean and*

*ironed; she has gray hair, her face that of a good woman. She is Algerian. When the children falter in their prayers, she helps them. When they have finished she says with an Algerian accent:*

SERVANT: Now, let's go to say good night.

*In the dining room, there is a large open window. The beach, the sea, and the sound of the surf are outside, not too distant. It is a starry night. At a table, there are four men and four women, all of them well dressed and tanned. It is the home of Henry and Bernadette Arnaud. The Assistant Commissioner is in plain clothes. He and his wife seem ill at ease, somewhat out of place.*
*The maid and children have entered the room.*

BERNADETTE: Come here, children. Say hello . . .

CHILDREN: Good evening . . .

*The others smile. The servant accompanies the children to their parents.*

CHILDREN: Good night, daddy. Good night, mommy.

BERNADETTE: Good night, dear. . . .

*They kiss. At the same time the women make the usual delighted exclamations. One of the men attracts the Assistant Commissioner's attention, points to his watch, and makes a sign.*
*The Assistant Commissioner nods his head affirmatively.*

SCENE **47**

ALGERIAN STREETS. OUTSIDE.
NIGHT.

*A DS Citroen is crossing the city at high speed.*
*The four men are inside. Arnaud is at the wheel. The Assistant Commissioner is sitting in the back seat.*

SCENE **48**

CASBAH ENTRANCE. OUTSIDE.
NIGHT.

*The automobile arrives at Place du Gouvernement, takes a turn around the square, then turns toward the blockade, and slows down.*
*One of the soldiers moves to the center of the ramp, and raises the phosphorescent flag. The car lowers its headlights and stops.*
*The soldier goes to the driver's window. In his right hand, he is holding a machine gun which hangs from his shoulders. He greets them.*
*He bends to window level:*

SOLDIER: Good evening . . .

*Arnaud responds in an innocent, cheerful tone:*

ARNAUD: Good evening . . . Can we pass? . . .

SOLDIER: It's too late. No one is allowed to enter the Casbah at this hour. It's impossible.

ARNAUD: But it's not even midnight yet!

SOLDIER: It's ten minutes past midnight. Curfew begins at midnight.

ARNAUD: Please, we just want to take a short ride. A friend of mine has never seen the Casbah.

SOLDIER: I'm sorry. Tomorrow. Tonight is out of the question.

*The Assistant Commissioner intervenes with the self-assured and somewhat arrogant tone common to all policemen. He stretches his arm toward the window and hands the soldier a card.*

ASSISTANT COMMISSIONER: It's alright, they're with me.

*The soldier examines the card by the glare of the headlights, hands it back, and bringing his hand to his visor, he salutes.*

SOLDIER: Okay, sir. Go ahead.

*The Assistant Commissioner salutes with his hand.*

ASSISTANT COMMISSIONER: Let's go, Henry.

ARNAUD (*he changes gears*): Thank you. Good evening.

*The soldier steps aside, and salutes again.*
*The automobile begins to move, steadily increasing its speed.*

SCENE 49
CASBAH STREET. OUTSIDE. NIGHT.

*The streets of the Casbah are deserted, almost completely blackened. Some cats are frightened by the headlights and run close to the walls.*

*Inside the car the four men are silent. They keep their eyes fixed straight ahead of them, their faces concentrating, taut.*

ARNAUD: This way?

ASSISTANT COMMISSIONER: Yes, it's the first intersection . . . or the second.

SCENE 50

RUE DE THEBES. OUTSIDE. NIGHT.

*The automobile slows down at the first intersection. Arnaud leans out the window and looks. There is an enamel nameplate—RUE DE THÈBES.*

ARNAUD: Right or left?

ASSISTANT COMMISSIONER: Try going to the right.

*The car turns right, moving slowly.*
*On one side of the street, the even numbers are getting higher: 26 . . . 28 . . . 30 . . .*

ARNAUD: What number is it?

ASSISTANT COMMISSIONER: Eight.

*The man next to the Assistant Commissioner says:*

FRIEND: Let's park here. It doesn't matter.

ASSISTANT COMMISSIONER (*in sharp tone*): It does matter. Go back, Henry. Let's go to number eight.

*Arnaud puts the gears in reverse; the car moves back quickly and passes the intersection: 16 . . . 14 . . . 12 . . . 10 . . . 8 . . . it stops.*
*Arnaud puts it in neutral. With the motor still running, he presses the cigarette lighter on the dashboard.*
*The Assistant Commissioner takes a large package that he is holding under his legs on the car floor. It is wrapped in pieces of newspaper. He lifts it forward. The man who is next to Arnaud takes it, leans it against the back of his seat, touches*

*it until he finds the right spot, unwraps it from that part, and straightens a small plastic tube which appears at the opening. It is a fuse.*

ARNAUD: How long do you want the timing device?

FRIEND: Five minutes. Give me a match . . .

*Arnaud takes the cigarette lighter from the dashboard.*

*The other man has opened the car door. He takes the lighter and touches it to the fuse which ignites immediately. The door of number eight is very near, almost directly opposite the car door.*

*The man places the package in a shady area and returns to the car in a run. Arnaud has already changed gears, releases the clutch, and the automobile shoots forward.*

## SCENE 51

RUE DE THÈBES. EXPLOSION. OUT-
SIDE. NIGHT. AUGUST 11, 1956.
12:20 A.M.

*The explosion is very violent. The fronts of buildings number eight, ten, and twelve explode and collapse.*
EXPLOSION.
*The echo of the explosion has ended. There is a long pause, only some isolated noises resound. They are stressed, recognizable: a burning beam, the thud of falling debris, broken glass . . .*
*Then suddenly and almost simultaneously with the other sounds, after the shock, the human voices, the shouts and weeping are heard.*
VOICES, SHOUTS, WEEPING.

## SCENE 52

RUE DE THÈBES. OUTSIDE. DAWN.

*The dawn's light is clear and white. It dispels every shadow and designs precisely every outline. Here and there, in the middle of the sky, there are numerous clouds of dust, strangely motionless. In the light, the human figures seem black. Seen from a distance, they seem to be ants upon heaps of debris. There are women, motionless, weeping softly, their voices similar to prayer. From time to time, there is a sudden scream, a despairing sob, someone running.*
*Another corpse is pulled out from the rubble, bodies mutilated or still intact—they are all dead.*
*The people continue to rummage through the debris and to wait around pitifully.*

SCENE 53
CASBAH STREETS. OUTSIDE. DAY.

*But there is no pity in the other streets and alleys of the Casbah, or at the top of the steps. There is anger and hatred.*
*The people are running and shouting.*
*They are shouting from their windows and balconies:*
JU-JU.
*They smother every other sound. The excitement increases.*
*They run where there is more shouting, more people. They don't know what to do yet, but want to be together. Until there is a voice stronger and clearer than the others which gives them a goal and direction.*
*Ali la Pointe points below beyond the slopes of the alleys and stairways. There below are the European quarters which widen near the sea.*
*The crowd is shouting, pushing, rushing forward with him, like a raging stream, tumultuous and unrestrainable.*
*Ali is together with his men, five boys, none of them older than twenty. All of them are armed. The crowd forces them to quicken their step to a run.*
*Petit Omar is furthest in the rear. He is wearing a pair of short pants, his chest bare; he is barefoot. He calls Ali with all his might, but in vain.*
*He tries to join Ali, to make his way through the legs of the others; he runs, clinging to the others, pushes, passes near the walls; then, turning into a side-street, he rushes into an alleyway, and finally arrives in front.*
*He runs to Ali, almost out of breath.*

PETIT OMAR (*shouting*): Kader says to stop them! He says we've got to stop them!

*Ali slows down as much as he can with the crowd pushing him from behind.*

ALI: Where's Kader?

PETIT OMAR: With the others. They are trying to stop the people.

ALI: Go away.

*Their voices can hardly be heard or understood amid the loud noises.*

PETIT OMAR: But he says that if we go on like this, we're playing their game, and they'll murder everyone . . . Stop, Ali!

*Ali continues to run. His face is sullen, frowning, as always when he must choose between instinct and reason.*

*Omar calls him again. His voice is hysterical, repeating again to stop. He is hanging on one of Ali's arms. Ali jerks himself free violently; he strikes the child. Omar sways and falls against the wall.*

*With this movement, Ali seems to release his anger at not being able to carry out his actions.*

*He slows down, speaks to his men, a few words in Arabic, his voice cold and bitter.*

*Ali extends his arm and the others imitate him. Each man grabs another by the arm, forming a chain. They check the flow behind them and hold back the crowd that is pressing forward.*

SCENE **54**

KADER'S HOUSE. INSIDE. DAY.
SEPTEMBER 30, 1956.

*Djamila, the girl who in January, in rue Random, gave the revolver to Ali la Pointe, is now standing in front of a large mirror. She removes the veil from her face. Her glance is hard and intense; her face is expressionless. The mirror reflects a large part of the room: it is a bedroom. There are three other girls.*

*There is Zohra, who is about the same age as Djamila. She undresses, removing her traditional costume, and is wearing a slip . . .*

*There is Hassiba who is pouring a bottle of peroxide into a basin. She dips her long black hair into the water to dye it blond.*

*Every action is performed precisely and carefully. They are*

*like three actresses preparing for the stage. But there is no*
*gaiety; no one is speaking. Only silence emphasizes the de-*
*tailed rhythm of their transformation . . .*
*Djamila's lightweight European dress of printed silk . . .*
*Zohra's blouse and short skirt to her knees . . . make-up,*
*lipstick, high-heeled shoes, silk stockings . . .*
*Hassiba has wrapped her hair in a towel to dry it . . . a*
*pair of blue jeans, a striped clinging tee-shirt . . .*
*Her blond hair is now dry. She ties it behind in a ponytail.*
*Hassiba has a young, slim figure. She seems to be a young*
*European girl who is preparing to go to the beach.*
*Continual silence. Djamila and Zohra have finished their*
*preparations and sit down to wait. Hassiba is still barefoot.*
*She is putting on her sandals, when someone knocks at the*
*door.*

*Djamila gets up and goes to open it.*
*It is Kader.*
*A quick attentive glance; Djamila . . . Zohra . . . Hassiba . . .*
*Hassiba responds to his look with a gay and somewhat coquettish expression; she says, stressing her French:*

HASSIBA: Ça va, monsieur?

*Kader smiles for a second, without any gaiety, but to please her. Then he speaks briefly and harshly in Arabic. And turning one at a time to each of the three, he gives them three addresses.*

KADER (*to Djamila*): Number three rue de Chêne.
  (*to Zohra*): Number fourteen rue Monseigneur Leynaud.
  (*to Hassiba*): Number twenty-one rue de l'Hydre.

*Each one of the girls repeats, in turn, the address which he has given her. Each one of the three responds emotionally. The atmosphere is tense. Kader bids them farewell according to the Algerian custom, first bringing his right hand over his heart. Then he embraces them.*
*They look at him for a moment; they are embarrassed. Kader tries to ease their discomfort, smiles, and answers Hassiba's previous remark.*

KADER: Ça va . . . Et bonnes chances!

SCENE 55

RUE DE L'HYDRE. OUTSIDE/INSIDE.
DAY. 5:45 P.M.

*At number twenty-one rue de l'Hydre, there is a bread store. Hassiba has again covered her face with a veil, and is also wearing a white cloak which covers her whole body.*
*She enters the store. There are other women who are buying bread. Hassiba waits for them to leave, then says in Arabic to the shopkeeper:*

HASSIBA: I've come to take the package . . .

*The shopkeeper empties half a basket of bread; at the bottom, there is a beach bag with a shoulder-strap, and he gives it to Hassiba.*
*Hassiba hides it under her cloak, bends her head in a sign of farewell, and leaves.*

SCENE 56
RUE MONS. LEYNAUD. INSIDE. DAY.
5:45 P.M.

*At number fourteen rue Monseigneur Leynaud, there is a tailor shop and clothing store. Zohra is also wearing the veil and white cloak. She enters.*

ZOHRA: I've come to take the package . . .

*The tailor accompanies her to the back of the shop, where there is a workroom and young girls who are sewing. He rummages in a closet, takes out an Air France utility bag and gives it to Zohra who hides it under her cloak, greets him, and leaves.*

SCENE 57
RUE DU CHÊNE. INSIDE. DAY.

*Inside number three rue du Chêne, an Algerian craftsman is working in filigree. Djamila takes a small leather cosmetic-case.*
*Djamila hides it, greets the man, and leaves.*

SCENE 58
ALLEY AND BLOCKADE. RUE
MARENGO. INSIDE/OUTSIDE. DAY.
6:05 P.M.

*At an intersection of rue Marengo, an alley, Hassiba enters a large door, and shuts it. In a second, she has removed her veil and cloak. Her face is made up; she is wearing pants and a jersey top. She places the strap of her bag on her shoulder.*

*Inside the bag, a towel and bathing suit are visible.*
*Hassiba goes out the door, proceeds down the alley until she reaches rue Marengo. She approaches the blockade.*
*It is Saturday evening; there is a hurried bustle of Algerians and Europeans. Soldiers and policemen are very busy with their usual requests for documents.*
*Hassiba's arrival is quickly noticed for she is very pretty and attracts much attention. Some soldiers whistle.*
*An elderly Algerian woman looks at her with dislike. Hassiba is indifferent and waits her turn. A French soldier approaches her.*

SOLDIER: I'd like to search you, Miss . . .

*For an instant, Hassiba is dismayed; then she glances down at her clinging shirt and pants.*

HASSIBA (*innocently*): Where?

*The boy is young, handsome, and cheeky.*

SOLDIER: Not here. There's too many people.

HASSIBA: But you don't understand. I was saying that there's nothing to search.

SOLDIER: That's what *you* think!

*Some Europeans laugh, the Algerians seem not to see or hear, but it is evident that they are scornful.*

SECOND SOLDIER: Are you going for a swim, Miss . . . all by yourself?

HASSIBA: No, with some friends.

*At the same time, she passes the blockade.*

SECOND SOLDIER: Lucky them. Next Sunday I'm free . . . Shall we go together?

*Hassiba shrugs her shoulders, smiles again, and moves away.*

## SCENE 59
### BLOCKADE RUE DU DIVAN.
### OUTSIDE. DAY.

*At the rue du Divan blockade, Zohra too is dressed like a European, and seems to be calm.*
*There are not too many people. A soldier makes a sign for her to pass in a hurried manner, and the girl passes.*

## SCENE 60
### BLOCKADE RUE DE LA LYRE.
### OUTSIDE. DAY.

*Djamila is tense, pale, her features are strained. Her eyes seem even larger with make-up. Now, at the blockade at rue de la Lyre the Casbah exit is blocked. An Algerian has been*

*discovered without documents. He argues, shouts, and says
that he wants to go back.*
INCOHERENT VOICES.
*The soldiers try to catch him, he struggles to get free.
Meanwhile the people push forward in protest. Two soldiers
catch the Algerian and drag him bodily into the guard posts.
The flow of people continues.
Djamila steps forward, holding the cosmetic-case with both
of her hands. She doesn't know how to carry it, and from time
to time she changes her position. She realizes that she looks
awkward.
It's now her turn. The soldiers' tone is arrogant. The previous
scene has made them nervous. An officer signals her to pass,
then points to the cosmetic-case.*

OFFICER: What's inside?

*Instinctively, Djamila lifts the case and looks at it; she feels
herself failing, but makes an effort to answer.*

DJAMILA: Here?

OFFICER: There . . .

*Djamila uses all her strength to smile and she succeeds. Her
eyes light up defiantly.*

DJAMILA (*provocatively*): Nothing.

*The officer signals her to pass.*


SCENE 61
FISH-MARKET. INSIDE. DAY.
6:15 P.M.

*A large warehouse in the fish-market. There are enormous ice-
boxes with cartons of frozen fish and tubs with running water
and live fish. The three girls are next to one another.
The three bags are on top of the counter, a few steps away.
With them is a thin Algerian about twenty-five years old. He
has thick black hair, straight and combed neatly. He is wear-*

*ing glasses. With his rough and nervous hands, he pulls out
the towel and bathing suit from Hassiba's bag, then delicately
and carefully, a square wooden box. He opens it, and turning
to the girl, signals her to move away a bit. The girl steps back.
In the box, there is a huge iron tube, sealed at both ends by
two clock dials. Inside the tube, two batteries with wires are
attached to the dials. The youth glances at his wristwatch,
then adjusts the hands of the dials to six forty-five. He puts*

*the bomb back into the box, closes it, and places it in the bag.
He replaces the towel and bathing suit, then hands the bag
to Hassiba. He is smiling slightly.
Hassiba takes the bag and goes away.
The box fits perfectly into Djamila's cosmetic-case. The youth
opens it without removing it from the case, adjusts the two
dials to six fifty, puts everything back in its place, and hands
the case to Djamila. He smiles at her and she moves away.
In the Air France bag, there are newspapers and magazines
on top, and the same box. The youth adjusts the bomb to six
fifty-five, arranges it again inside the bag, closes the zipper,
and hands the bag to Zohra. He smiles at her. His smile is
more genuine, less mechanical. There is less tension than
before.
The youth smiles at the girl and says in Arabic:*

ALGERIAN: May Allah protect you.

*Zohra thanks him in a whisper, bends her head, and moves
away. The youth takes a cigarette from his shirt pocket, places
it between his lips, and lights it. His hand is trembling a little.*

SCENE 62

CAFETERIA RUE MICHELET. INSIDE.
DAY. 6:30 P.M.

*Cafeteria, rue Michelet 1. The club is very crowded. There
are two rooms; one at the entrance with an American-style
bar, and one at the back with tables. It is Saturday, and at
this hour many European families go out to have an ice
cream. There is not too much confusion or uproar. The people
are calm, they take their places at the bar and small tables,
and eat their ice cream while chatting quietly.
Hassiba enters, glances at the large clock above the cash
register. It is half past six. She goes to the register and waits
her turn. The different orders mingle; she orders a Coca-
Cola. They give her the check. She pays.
She goes to the bar; all the seats are taken. She gives her
order and the ticket to the waiter.*

*A man moves aside, looks at her, then steps down from his*
*stool and offers it to her.*
*Hassiba tells him that it doesn't matter, but the man insists.*
*Hassiba thanks him and sits down. The man is about fifty,*
*well groomed. He smiles again, and turns to chat with some*
*friends.*
*Hassiba settles herself more comfortably on the seat, then*
*removes the bag from her shoulder. Holding it by the strap,*

*she places it on the floor below the counter behind the brass
railing used to lean one's feet.
The waiter has brought her the drink. Hassiba drinks slowly,
from time to time glancing at the clock. She finishes drinking.
The bag is in a vertical position.
Moving her feet slowly and carefully, Hassiba lets the bag
slip on its side.
She gets down from the seat, and points it out to the man who
is standing next to her.*

HASSIBA: I'm giving your seat back.

MAN: Are you already leaving, Miss?

*Hassiba smiles, nods yes.*

HASSIBA: Good evening . . .

*The man sits down.*

MAN: Good evening . . .

SCENE 63

MILK BAR. RUE D'ISLY. OUTSIDE/
INSIDE. DAY.

*Milk Bar, rue d'Isly, at the corner of Place Bugeand. The
jukebox is playing full blast. It is a bar for young people.
There is much bustle and confusion, much laughter. The girls
are making plans for Sunday.
Djamila enters and moves to the jukebox which is in the
corner near the door. There are playbills for various theater
performances hanging on the wall. Djamila stops to look at
them and reads the bottom lines. She places the cosmetic-case
on the floor. Rising again she looks around her, and pushes
the case behind the jukebox with her foot . . .*

SCENE 64

AIR FRANCE. IMMEUBLE MAURE-
TANIA. INSIDE. DAY.

*Maison Blanche, Immeuble Mauretania. The entire ground
floor is filled with ticket counters and a waiting room for the*

*airlines. There are some employees, stewardesses and some travelers.*

*Zohra passes through the large glass door at the entrance, goes to the Air France counter, takes a time schedule, then goes to sit down on a sofa which runs along the opposite wall. She sits down and places the airline bag on the ground in front of her, and begins to leaf through the timetable, from time to time glancing around. Using her heels, she pushes the bag under the sofa.*

*She looks at the large electric clock which is hanging in the center of the room; it is forty minutes past six.*

SCENE 65

CAFETERIA RUE MICHELET.
INSIDE. DAY.

*It is six forty-four by the cafeteria clock. The second hand is moving.*
*There are more or less the same people. The old man is still seated on the barstool, and continues to chat.*
*Hassiba's bag is still at his feet; the second hand is racing.*
*A five-year-old child hands a coin to the waiter:*

CHILD: Ice cream . . .

*The father and mother are watching him, delighted.*
*The waiter smiles at the child and points to the cash register. He speaks to the child in the usual tone of a grownup when speaking to children:*

WAITER: You have to go there first . . . and then come back to me.

*The second hand reaches twenty-five, then thirty. The child goes to the cashier and pays. The cashier smiles at him and gives him the check.*

CASHIER: What a good boy . . .

*The child returns to the counter. The waiter has already prepared the ice cream for him, and hands it to him. The child is standing on tiptoes.*

SCENE **66**

CAFETERIA MICHELET. EXPLOSION.
INSIDE. DAY.

*The second hand, the explosion: bodies flung into the air,
arms, legs, white smoke, screams.*
*Bodies thrown outside, the doors unhinged, the windows
broken, empty.*
*The people watch from their windows, the passersby move
closer, they bend down to look at those who are writhing on
the ground.*
*Astonished and incredulous faces. No one speaks. Only
screams and weeping. Sirens which are drawing nearer. Fire-
men and police arriving . . .*

SCENE **67**

MILK BAR. RUE D'ISLY. OUTSIDE.
DAY.

*The ambulance sirens on rue d'Isly, one car after another.*
*At the Milk Bar, the people go to the doors to look at the
ambulances which are racing toward Place Bugeand. The
sirens fade in the distance and move away. The jukebox is
again loud: "Brigitte Bardot, Bardot . . ."*
*The people re-enter the bar, chattering, to have their apéritifs.
It is six fifty: the explosion.*

SCENE **68**

MILK BAR. EXPLOSION. OUTSIDE.
DAY.

*The jukebox is flung into the middle of the street. There is
blood, strips of flesh, material, the same scene as at the Cafeteria; the white smoke and shouts, weeping, hysterical girls'*

*screams. One of them no longer has an arm and runs around,
howling despairingly; it is impossible to control her. The
sound of sirens is heard again. The crowd of people, the fire-
men, police, ambulances all rush to the scene from Place
Bugeand.*

*The ambulances arrive at rue Michelet.*

*They are already loaded with dead and wounded. The rela-
tives of the wounded are forced to get out. The father of the
child who was buying ice cream seems to be in a daze: he
doesn't understand.*

*They pull him down by force. The child remains there, his
blond head a clot of blood.*

*The policemen try to bring order to the chaos, are forced to
shout, push, threaten. The wounded swarm around the ambulances. A Commissioner sends off the first one.*

COMMISSIONER: What time is it?

POLICEMAN: A quarter to seven.

*The Commissioner goes to the second ambulance, pulls down
a man who is trying to enter by force, slams the door, and
shouts to the driver. His face is pale and drawn; the veins of
his neck are swollen.*

COMMISSIONER: Go away, for God's sake!

*The auto leaves and now, the third explosion resounds in the
distance. It is heard clearly and violently from the Mauretania section.*

*The Commissioner stops midway in his last gesture, and like-
wise, all the others, who are paralyzed with fright, incapable
of taking action again, of accepting such reality for a third
time.*

*In Place Bugeand, there also, the people are motionless. All
of them are looking in the same direction. Their faces are
alike in their terror, alike in their sense of impotence, alike
in their deep sadness.*

SCENE 69

STREET. EUROPEAN CITY. OUTSIDE.
DAY.

*The sun appears, then hides behind black clouds. There is a
cool wind. It is ten in the morning, and the European city has
its usual rapid and efficient rhythm of every day at this hour,
only there is terror written on the face of every person. That
same terror has remained, and suspicion, and despairing impotence.*
*Patrols of soldiers and policemen move around the city,
search Algerians and some Europeans, stop automobiles,
trucks, buses, and trams that they block at both doors.*
*At the entrance to every shop, the owner searches every cus-
tomer before letting him enter.*
*He does so politely with a drawn smile, and methodically
rummages through every handbag, every package.*
*So too in the bars, in the offices, in workshops . . . And now
that it is already late afternoon, also outside the brothels, the
cinemas, the theaters.*

SCENE 70

LEMONS STREET. OUTSIDE. SUNSET.

*A young Algerian boy, thirteen or fourteen years old, wearing
sandals, without socks, trousers that reach to his ankles, walks
quickly carrying a cardboard box tied with a cord. It is dusk.
A European woman sees him pass in front of her, looks at
him, and follows him with her glance.*
*On the sidewalk there are some youths. The woman points to
the Algerian boy, says something. The traffic is heavy. Her
words are unclear. One youth calls to the boy who is by now
thirty feet away:*

YOUTH: Hey, little rat . . .

*The boy turns around for a second, his face frightened, and quickens his step. The youths follow behind him and the boy begins to run. The youths too begin to run and others join them, people who are passing. They form a small mob and are shouting. The boy shoots into a side-street, drops his box, and races ahead.*

*While some chase the boy, others stop around the box, make way, look for a policeman, a soldier, an officer. A circle continues to form around the box. A patrol arrives. One of the soldiers has a geiger counter. He moves near the box, carefully placing the counter above it, then ceasing to be prudent, he takes his bayonette, cuts the cord, and tears open the box: lemons.*

SCENE 71

STREET CORNER. OUTSIDE. SUNSET.

*The boy has been cornered, surrounded, pinned down, kicked, hit with umbrellas, until he is exhausted and can no longer defend himself. He is no longer moving. He is lying on the ground, dead. The air is gray now, and slowly all the colors unite to form gray. Lights are lit in the city and contrast with the whiteness of the Casbah high above. The sky is still clear, the black profiles of the mountains, the straight coasts on the sea, the sea itself that seems to be land until it reaches the horizon where the moon rises between the clouds.*

SPEAKER: "Following a lengthy discussion, the General Assembly of the United Nations has decided its agenda for the forthcoming debates:

(1) re-unification of Korea
(2) disarmament
(3) the Algerian question.

Colombia has proposed that only the first two points be discussed for the day. However, the Afro-Asian nations opposed, underlining the importance they attribute to the Algerian question . . ."

SCENE 72

SEA-FRONT. OUTSIDE. DAY.
JANUARY 10, 1957.

*The European crowd applauds, their eyes aglow, their mouths
wide open, shouting and yelling, their teeth flashing in the
sun. Clapping of applause on the sea-front of Algiers. Children are held up to see, waving small flags. The paratroopers
of the Tenth Division march past.*

SPEAKER: "Mr. Raymond Lefevre, Inspector General of the Administration, has presided over a meeting in which important de-
cisions have been taken with the aim of securing public order
and the protection of persons and their property. In particular,
it has been decided to recall the 'Tenth' Division of paratroopers
to Algiers that, until now, has been employed in the antiguerrilla
operations on the Cabiro plateau. The Commander General of the
Tenth Division will assume responsibility for the maintenance of
order in Algiers, and will have at his disposal in order to achieve
this goal, all civil and military means provided for the defense of
the zone."

*Massu and the authorities are standing on the balconies of the
Prefecture building.*
*The paras are marching, their sleeves rolled up, their faces
sunburned. Machine guns, bazookas, crew-cuts, the eyes of
singing boys, silent steps, one battalion after another.*
*The dragon "black berets" pass by . . .*
*The "red berets" of the 2nd Regiment of colonial paratroop-
ers . . .*
*"Les casquettes" of the 3rd Regiment parade by; "les
hommes-peints," Mathieu's paras.*
*Colonel Mathieu is at the head of the regiment. He is tall,
slender, over fifty. He has thinning gray hair, a lean face,
blue eyes, and a wide forehead. His face is lined with many
wrinkles. Were it not for the uniform, the weapons, his tanned
skin, his manner of walking, and his energetic voice when
giving orders, he wouldn't seem a soldier, but an intellectual.*

*The 3rd Regiment colonial paratroopers are now before the Commissioner. Mathieu turns his head slightly and:*

MATHIEU: 3rd Regiment! Attention à droite . . . Droite!

SPEAKER:

FAMILY NAME: Mathieu

NAME: Philippe
Born in Rennes May 3, 1906

RANK: Lieutenant Colonel

SCHOOLING: Politechnique—degree in Engineering

CAMPAIGNS: Second World War, Anti-Nazi Resistance Movement, Italian Campaign, Indochinese War, Algerian War . . .

SCENE 73

VILLA HEADQUARTERS. INSIDE. DAY.

*In a villa in the military headquarters, a reception room is visible through a large window on the first floor. There are about twenty officers seated in rows of chairs as if for a lecture. Mathieu is in front of them and he is speaking while standing next to a desk. At his back there is a blackboard, and near it, a large map with pyramid graphs, cells, arrows, crossmarks, and, above them, the title:* STRUCTURE NLF AUTONOMOUS ZONE OF ALGIERS.

*Mathieu's voice has nothing of the military and traditional. His tone is neither harsh nor cold, but rather kind and pleasing; from it emanates a superior authority imposed by reason and not by position.*

MATHIEU: The result is that in the last two months, they have reached an average of 4.2 assaults per day, including aggression against individuals, and the explosions. Of course, the conditions of the problem are as usual: first, the adversary; second, the method to destroy him . . . There are 80,000 Arabs in the Casbah. Are they all against us? We know they are not. In reality, it is only a small minority that dominates with terror and violence. This minority is our adversary and we must isolate and destroy it . . .

*While speaking, he goes to the window, and pulls down the shade. He interrupts his speech, points to the rest of the window:*

MATHIEU: Draw it down there too . . .

*Two or three officers stand up to perform the task. At the back of the room there is a movie projector.*
*Next to it there is a* para *who is preparing to operate it.*
*The other shades are drawn, and gradually the room is darkened.*
*Mathieu, meanwhile, has resumed speaking:*

MATHIEU: He is an adversary who shifts his position above and below the surface with highly commendable revolutionary methods and original tactics. . . . He is an anonymous and unrecognizable enemy who mingles with thousands of others who resemble him. We find him everywhere: in the alleys of the Casbah; in the streets of the European city, and in working places. . . .

*Mathieu interrupts himself again and makes a signal to the back of the room which is completely darkened.*

MATHIEU: Go ahead, Martin.

*Martin turns on the projector. On the white wall next to the map and graph appear pictures of the Casbah. There are the blockades, the barbed wire, the metal screens, the Algerians who exit and enter, the policemen and soldiers who examine documents and frisk someone. From time to time, close-ups of the pictures are shown, enlarged to the minutest details, close-ups of faces, motionless images that last only for a few seconds.*

MATHIEU: Here is some film taken by the police. The cameras were hidden at the Casbah exits. They thought these films might be useful, and in fact they are useful in demonstrating the usefulness of certain methods. Or, at least, their inadequacy.

*Hassiba is now seen and the soldiers who are wooing her, while she laughs, jokes, flirts in a provocative manner, and passes the blockade.*

MATHIEU: I chose these films because they were shot in the hours preceding some recent terroristic assaults. And so, among all these Arabs, men and women, there are the ones responsible. But which ones are they? How can we recognize them? Controlling documents is ridiculous: one who has everything in order is most likely to be the terrorist.

*An Algerian is being dragged away while protesting, kicking, and trying to free himself. And then the scene changes. There is another Casbah exit, and an Algerian who is being searched.*

MATHIEU (*smiling*): Note the intuition of the camera-man. He realized that in that box, there had to be something of interest, and he paused to focus it.

*The picture is enlarged. The small box which the Algerian is carrying on his shoulder is seen in detail. It is opened. The box is swarming with snakes; the soldier who had wanted to examine it jumps backward.*
*The officers in the room burst into laughter.*

MATHIEU (*laughing*): Maybe the bomb was hidden right there, in a double bottom. Who knows? We'll never know.

*Using the barrel of his machine gun, a soldier has closed the box. A snake has managed to jump out, and fallen to the ground. The people are terrified and move away. Others laugh, among them, Petit Omar, who seems to be an ordinary child enjoying himself.*

MATHIEU: That's enough, Martin . . .

*The lights are again switched on in the room. Mathieu is again next to the desk, and waits a second until the buzz of comments subsides.*

MATHIEU: We must start again from scratch. The only information that we have concerns the structure of the organization. And we shall begin from that . . .

*He takes a wooden pointer from the desk in order to illustrate the graph, while he speaks with the tone and precision of a university professor.*

MATHIEU: It is a pyramid-like organization divided into a series of sectors. At the top of the pyramid is their General Staff.

*He has moved near the blackboard, and taken some chalk, and slowly as he speaks, he illustrates his speech.*

MATHIEU: The military commander responsible for the executive body finds the right man and nominates him to responsibility for a sector: number one. Number one in his turn, chooses another two: number two and number three . . . And so they form the first triangle.

*He has written high on the board a number one, and below it, with some space between them, the numbers two and three.*
*He unites the three numbers with lines and forms a triangle.*

MATHIEU: Now number two and number three choose, in their turn, two men each . . . number four and five, and so on . . .

*Mathieu writes the new numbers, spacing them on the next line. Then he unites two to four and five, and three to six and seven, forming two new triangles.*
*Mathieu has written other numbers and unites them to those of the preceding line and thus forms other triangles.*
*Now the blackboard is covered by a series of triangles that form a large pyramid.*

MATHIEU: The reason for this geometry is so that every militant will know only three members in the entire organization: his commander who has chosen him, and the two members that he himself has chosen . . . Contacts take place only by written instructions . . . That is why we do not know our adversaries: because, in practice, they do not even know each other.

*Mathieu leaves the blackboard and moves near the officers. The tone of his voice changes. The explanation is now finished. He gives directions . . .*

MATHIEU: To know them means to eliminate them. Consequently, the military aspect is secondary to the police method. I know we are not fond of this word, but it is the only word that indicates exactly the type of work that we must perform. We must make the necessary investigations in order to proceed from one vertex to another in the entire pyramid. The reason for this work is information. The method is interrogation. And interrogation becomes a method when conducted in a manner so as to always obtain a result, or rather, an answer. In practice, demonstrating a false humanitarianism only leads to the ridiculous and to impotence. I am certain that all the units will understand and react accordingly. However, success does not depend solely on us. We need to have the Casbah at our disposal. We must sift through it . . . and interrogate everyone. And here is where we find ourselves hindered by a conspiracy of laws and regulations that continue to be operative, as if Algiers were a holiday resort and not a battleground. We have requested a carte blanche. But it is very difficult to obtain. Therefore, it is necessary to find an excuse to legitimize our intervention, and make it possible. It is necessary to create it ourselves—this excuse. Unless our adversaries will think of it themselves, which seems to be what they are doing.

SCENE 74

ALLEY UPPER CASBAH. OUTSIDE.
DAY.

*It is not a song, but a type of spoken chorus, an assembly of young voices, words whispered from the throat, both high and low, and sudden silent pauses. It is monotonous; but it is just such a repetition, always with the same pattern of tones— high, low, then silent—that manages to transform itself into a motif, reach an excited pitch, and acquire breadth and solemnity. The sound fills the alleys, rises toward the long rectangle of sky, and moves farther away as if it were meant to be heard by all.*
*The alley is narrow and sloping, with crumbling walls, tufts of grass, and refuse. It is located at the outer periphery of the Casbah—the countryside is in the background. An Algerian is walking with large steps; a five-year-old child is behind him, moving quickly, stumbling from time to time on the pavement; although he does not cry, occasionally he calls to his father, who proceeds forward, and does not turn around. The chorus arises from behind them. It is incoherent. They stop in front of a door; they have arrived. The door gives way and they enter.*

SCENE 75

KORAN SCHOOL. INSIDE. DAY.

*A large room, like a shop or stable. Here too, on the ground and pavement, there are tufts of grass. It is cold. The walls are unplastered, the windows boarded. The roof is in sight, but not the beams. The roof is made of tiles and covered with a coat of whitewash.*
*There are about twenty children, five to eight years old, seated on the floor. The teacher is in front of them; he too is seated. He is prompting the verses in a low voice, almost in a whisper, and the chorus repeats it.*

*The Koran School: a bare, wobbling place.*
*The Algerian who has entered takes the child by his hand, and*
*accompanies him to the teacher who is now standing; the*
*chorus continues; the other children do not look at the two*
*who have just entered.*
*The Algerian and the teacher greet each other, bringing their*
*hands to their hearts, and then to their mouths. At the same*
*time, the teacher takes an envelope from under his tunic, and*
*hands it over to the other.*

SPEAKER: "To all militants! After two years of hard struggle in
the mountains and city, the Algerian people have obtained a great
victory. The UN Assembly has placed the Algerian question in its
forthcoming agenda. The discussion will begin on Monday, January 28. Starting Monday, for a duration of eight days, the NLF
is calling a general strike. For the duration of this period, all
forms of armed action or attempts at such are suspended. We are
requesting that all militants mobilize for the strike's organization
and success."

*The Algerian has hidden the envelope inside his tunic, then*
*presents the child to the teacher, who makes him sit down*
*with the other children. The teacher also returns to his place*
*and sits down, and suggests a new phrase; the chorus con-*
*tinues. The Algerian leaves the school.*

SCENE **76**
ALLEY UPPER CASBAH. OUTSIDE.
DAY.

*Having passed through the door, he again moves along the*
*alley, this time descending, with hurried steps. The chorus*
*continues, again heard from without, but its echo is now*
*different . . .*

SCENE 77

VARIOUS VIEWS CASBAH. OUTSIDE/
INSIDE. DAY.

*Bars, stores, market stalls, "Arab baths." Typewritten pieces
of paper are used to wrap purchases, or slipped inside bags,
or used on the blank side to add up bills and then handed to
the customers.*

SCENE 78

VARIOUS VIEWS EUROPEAN CITY.
OUTSIDE/INSIDE. DAY.

*In the European city the Algerian workers: at the docks, the
central gas company; on the trams; the waiters in the restau-
rants, in the bars; the shoeshine men . . .*

SPEAKER: "Algerian brothers! A great hope has arisen for us. The
world is watching us. The next few days may be decisive for our
future and our freedom. The colonial powers will attempt to
demonstrate to the UN that the NFL does not represent the will of
our people. Our response will be unanimous support of the general
strike."

SCENE 79

SEA-FRONT. OUTSIDE. DAY.

*At the sea-front, there is a newspaper boy, about twelve years
old, barefoot. His voice is shrill yet cheerful. He is smiling.*

NEWSBOY: *Le Monde! Le Monde!* General strike! . . . Strike! . . .

*Some Europeans buy the newspaper, half-heartedly, grum-
bling disagreeably. The boy remains cheerful, places the
change inside the bag strapped to his shoulder, thanks them.*

*Now he passes in front of a beggar, an elderly Algerian who is leaning against a railing.*
*The boy winks at him, while he continues to shout:*

NEWSBOY: Strike!

SPEAKER: "During the eight days of the strike, do not frequent the European city, or leave the Casbah. Provide lodgings in your homes for the poor, the beggars, the brothers who do not have homes. Store provisions of food and water for eight days!"

SCENE **80**

CASBAH STREETS AND SHOPS.
INSIDE/OUTSIDE. DAY.

*There is a strange atmosphere in the Casbah. People are greeting each other in the streets; a thick buzz of voices, a festive mood, a sense of brotherhood, and the children who are taking advantage of the situation and play and run everywhere.*
*The shops are unusually crowded. The people enter and exit, loaded with supplies. In the shops too, there is the same festive mood, almost as if the supplies were for a trip to the country. The shopkeepers are also cheerful.*
*And the poor customers, instead of paying, hand over a ticket stamped NLF.*

SCENE **81**

CASBAH BLOCKADE. OUTSIDE. DAY.
SUNSET. SUNDAY. JANUARY 27, 1957.

*Late afternoon, at the blockades of rue de la Lyre, rue du Divan, and rue Marengo. The Casbah exit ramps are deserted, while the entrance ramps are overflowing with people. Here too, there is an intangible air of gaiety, witty remarks, laughter, ironic glances toward the soldiers and policemen with cold faces, immobile—helmets and machine guns—who stand at the entrances without intervening.*

*The image is shortened and focused through the lenses of binoculars.*

SCENE 82

GOVERNMENT PALACE. OUTSIDE/
INSIDE. SUNSET.

*A paratrooper officer looks at the blockades of rue du Divan from a Government Palace balcony.*
*Mathieu is beside him.*

MATHIEU: No one is leaving, eh?

*The officer hands him the binoculars.*

OFFICER: No. They continue to enter, the rats.

*Mathieu looks through the binoculars, and comments in a low voice, smiling:*

MATHIEU: Rats in a trap, we hope . . .

OFFICER: But do you believe that the strike will be widespread?

MATHIEU: Without a doubt.

*Behind the two officers, through a large open window, a room is visible. There is a large table, and around it, other high officers of the various armed forces, and some important officials in plainclothes.*
*A general, who has his back to the balcony, turns and calls Mathieu:*

GENERAL: Mathieu! Mathieu, a name . . .

MATHIEU: A name?

GENERAL: Yes, a name for the operation.

*Mathieu moves the binoculars from the blockades and turns slowly around the Government square, until he reaches an advertising sign for a brand of champagne which now, in the dusk, lights up with a sporadic rhythm: CORDON . . . ROUGE.*

*Mathieu pauses then turns toward the room, and enters smiling:*

MATHIEU: Champagne . . . All right?

*The general repeats absent-mindedly:*

GENERAL: Champagne . . . Champagne.

(*then, in a convinced voice*)

Operation Champagne, yes, alright.

SCENE **83**

RUE DU DIVAN BLOCKADE. OUTSIDE.
EVENING.

*At the rue du Divan blockade, there is an incoherent, monotonous, and irritating chant. There is a blind beggar. He is light-complexioned, tall and thin, his beard long, his arms stretched out, a cane in his hand. He arrives at last at the entrance ramp, tries to find the way, but cannot.*
*He tries again and again with his cane, continually repeating his sorrowful chant, until a policeman takes him by his free hand, placing the hand roughly on the metal screen.*

POLICEMAN: Go on! Go on!

*The beggar protests and waves his cane in a way that the policeman has to duck to prevent himself from being hit.*
*The policeman curses, spitefully, coarsely.*
*A soldier starts to laugh. The old man takes up his chant again, and moves forward leaning on the metal screen.*
*On the other side of the blockade, behind the square, there is a group of veiled girls who have seen the old man, and seem to be waiting for him.*
*Two of them go to meet him, and each one takes one of his arms. At the touch of their hands, the old man is again infuriated. Even the girls laugh. Then one of them speaks to him slowly in a loud voice.*
*It seems that the old man has understood. He is convinced. He mumbles something kindly and lets them accompany him.*

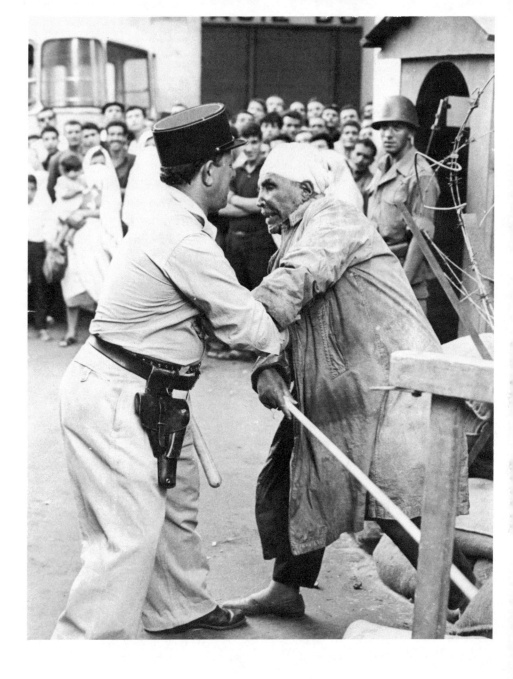

# SCENE 84

CASBAH ALLEY. FRONT DOOR. OUT-
SIDE. NIGHT.

> *A poorly lit alley. A group of unemployed men and beggars
> are standing in front of a door.*
> *One of the three companions consults a list, then points to two
> in the group. He signals them to enter.*

# SCENE 85

KADER'S HOUSE. INSIDE. NIGHT.

> *Inner courtyard.*
>
> *In the inner courtyard, there is an elderly man who awaits
> them and receives them kindly.*
> *They greet each other in the customary Algerian manner.*
>
> *Courtyard and balcony.*
>
> *On the terrace also, someone is looking toward the courtyard.
> Kader is on the terrace together with a man about forty years
> old, dressed in European clothes, he has narrow shoulders
> and a sunken chest. His face is sensitive, his forehead high,
> and his hair and eyes black. His eyes are kind and thoughtful
> and twinkle with irony.*
> *He is Ben M'Hidi, one of the four members of the CCE, the
> Central Executive Committee.*

KADER (*to him*): They are beggars and unemployed, homeless.
We have organized things in such a way that during the strike they
will be guests of other families who have homes and will provide
shelter in the event of possible reprisals . . . But I didn't know
that they would be brought to this house too. It is a mistake.

BEN M'HIDI: Why?

KADER: Because you are here too. It would be better for you to
move to another house.

*Ben M'Hidi moves away from the parapet.*

BEN M'HIDI: All right. You're the one who must decide.

*Kader follows him along the terrace.*

KADER: No, if I were the one to decide, you wouldn't be in Algiers now.

*Ben M'Hidi looks at him, smiling.*

BEN M'HIDI: Why? Isn't it wise?

*Kader smiles too, and repeats:*

KADER: It isn't wise.

> *At the end of the terrace, there is a construction raised to a level with the stairs that lead to the floor below. There is a large room; through the open door, the lighted interior is visible. The walls have high brick baseboards, and at the bottom of one of the four walls there is a square opening that leads into a hiding place. The closure of the hiding place, a square of very thick wall, is placed to one side. Ali la Pointe is covering it with bricks.*
> *On the other side of the room next to the door, there are some cement wash-basins, and a shed for rain water. Kader appears at the door.*

KADER: Ali, you must accompany Ben M'Hidi to the Maison des Arbres.

*Ali doesn't answer immediately. He finishes placing the last brick then turns to Kader.*

ALI: Why? Isn't he sleeping here?

KADER: No, it's better if he doesn't. The house is filled with new people.

*Ali gets up, wipes his hands on his trousers, at the same time inspecting the work that he has just completed.*

ALI: Here's another one ready. What a hideout! It really looks like a wall. I'll dirty it a bit, and it's perfect. Want to give a look inside?

*Kader has taken a machine gun from one of the basins, and he tosses it to Ali, who catches it.*

KADER: No, go now. It's already late.

*They go out on the terrace. Ali releases the catch of his machine gun so that the bullet slips into the barrel.*

KADER (*to Ben M'Hidi*): They are a family of militants from way back. Everything will work out well, you'll see . . . C'mon, Ali, hurry up.

BEN M'HIDI: Alright. See you tomorrow.

*They say good-bye, embracing one another. Ali has already climbed over the terrace wall, and has jumped to the next one.*
*Ben M'Hidi follows him; he is less agile and moves with a bit of trouble.*
*From the parapet, Kader says to him:*

KADER: Passing along the terraces only takes five minutes . . . and with Ali la Pointe, you'll be safe . . .

*While jumping, Ben M'Hidi loses his balance, and has to grab on to Ali to prevent himself from falling.*

BEN M'HIDI: But it's he who won't be safe with me . . .

*The two figures move away from terrace to terrace, and disappear in the dark.*

SCENE **86**

CASBAH VIEWS AND TERRACES.
OUTSIDE. NIGHT.

*In the dark in front of them, a metallic reflection is visible and the sharp and aggressive sound of an Algerian voice is heard.*
*Ali responds to the password.*
*A youth steps out from the shadows. He too is carrying a machine gun, recognizes Ali, and greets him. Ali and Ben M'Hidi continue . . .*

SCENE 87

MAISON DES ARBRES, TERRACE.
OUTSIDE. NIGHT.

*Until they arrive at a terrace which is separated from the next
one by an alley about ten feet wide.*

ALI: Here it is . . . We've arrived . . .

*Ben M'Hidi glances at the emptiness beneath them, looks at
Ali, and takes a deep breath.*

BEN M'HIDI: Not yet . . .

*Ali has climbed onto the parapet, looks around him concen-
trating attentively for a moment, and then jumps into the void,
reaching the opposite side. He bends, searches for something
in the dark, and lifts a type of gangplank.
He hands it over to Ben M'Hidi, and together they place it between the two terraces.*

ALI: Be careful now. Unless you know how it works, it's better if
you sit on the plank and move forward like this . . .

BEN M'HIDI: Let's try . . .

*He tries to stand up on the gangplank, but he lacks the neces-
sary steadiness. He can't hold his balance. He does as Ali has
advised him; he sits astride on the plank, and using the force
of his arms, he pushes himself forward.
He stops halfway to rest for a minute.*

BEN M'HIDI: It's good nobody is following us . . .

ALI: It's a question of habit . . .

*And when Ben M'Hidi is closer, Ali helps him to get down to
the terrace.*

ALI: It's better if I go first, to make sure everything's okay . . .

*Without waiting for an answer, he moves toward the stairway
that leads to the floor below; his movements are silent and
graceful.
Ben M'Hidi leans out from the terrace, and looks toward the*

*European city and the sea. At the port, two searchlights are
lit, and their long bright rays move slowly toward the Casbah . . .*
*When Ali la Pointe returns, Ben M'Hidi is still leaning on the
railing. He seems not to hear the sound of Ali's footsteps, or
his voice.*

ALI: Everything's okay . . . They're waiting for you . . .

*Ali moves near him, and Ben M'Hidi turns and looks at him.*

BEN M'HIDI: What do you think of the strike, Ali?

ALI: I think it'll be a success . . .

BEN M'HIDI: Yes, I think so too . . . It's been organized well . . .
But what will the French do?

*Both the question and the answer seem obvious to Ali.*

ALI (*shrugging*): It's clear. They'll do everything possible to make
it fail.

BEN M'HIDI: No, they'll do even more. We've given them the opportunity to do a lot more . . . Do you understand what I mean?
Starting tomorrow, they won't be groping in the dark any more;
every shop and every worker who strikes will be a known enemy, a
self-confessed criminal . . . And they will be able to pass to the
offensive. Have you thought of this?

*Ali has listened attentively. The effort with which he is trying
to ask himself the meaning of these words is visible on his
face.*

ALI (*shaking his head*): No . . .

BEN M'HIDI: But Kader told me that you weren't in favor of the
strike.

ALI: No, and neither were my men.

BEN M'HIDI: Why?

ALI: Because they told us that we mustn't use weapons, now, when
the time is right.

BEN M'HIDI: That's true . . . Wars aren't won with terrorism, neither wars nor revolutions. Terrorism is a beginning but afterward, all the people must act . . . This is the reason for the strike, and its necessity: to mobilize all Algerians, count them and measure their strength . . .

ALI: To show them to the UN, right?

BEN M'HIDI (*smiling slightly*): Yes . . . yes. The problem also involves the UN. I don't know what it's worth, but this way, we'll give the UN the possibility of evaluating our strength.

*Ali breathes deeply, instinctively, unrestrainedly, Ben M'Hidi watches him, smiles, and says:*

BEN M'HIDI: Do you know something Ali? Starting a revolution is hard, and it's even harder to continue it. Winning is hardest of all. But only afterward, when we have won, will the real hardships begin.

*He pats Ali's back fondly with his hand and continues, smiling:*

BEN M'HIDI: Anyway, there's still a lot to be done . . . you aren't already tired, Ali, are you?

*Ali looks at him, and without reacting to his irony:*

ALI (*with conviction*): No!

SCENE 88
VARIOUS HOUSES. CASBAH. OUTSIDE.
DAWN. JANUARY 28, 1957.

*It is gray and smoky dawn, a slow reabsorption of the night, an opaque light which is diffused, sprayed, frozen to transparency, and rediscovers its outlines and perspectives; and finally, the sun, golden light, awakens all Algiers. To the north, the sea. To the south, the mountains and the Casbah, situated halfway along the coast. The Casbah, still, inert, expectant, on this first day of the strike . . .*
*The paratroopers are already at their places, one after another, at equal distances like links of a very long chain, strung through every alley, spreading to every sidestreet, twisting*

*through the squares, climbing up the stairways, dividing, re-joining, and lengthening again. The silence is perfect; the camouflaged immobile forms seem to be part of the land-scape.*
*Then a brief and sharp hiss, a hundred whistles together.*
*A signal releases the still forms: the attack begins.*
*Doors are beaten down, shots, screams, rifle fire, machine-gun fire, the doors opened or broken down; the courtyards, the houses, the rooms, invaded; the men who are trying to escape and who protest and try to save themselves.*

VOICES: Of course . . . I was just going to work . . .

SCENE **89**

BEN M'HIDI'S HIDING PLACE.
INSIDE. DAWN.

*Ben M'Hidi is inside the hiding place. From outside, an old man helps him to place the square piece of wall over the en-trance, and then, in the spaces between the bricks, he adds a paste of plaster mixed with coal dust. When the* paras *arrive, everything is in order.*
*Still men are being seized, beaten, dragged; a cache of weap-ons; men pushed down the stairs:*

SOLDIERS: Go on, go on, you little rats! Get to work!

SCENE **90**

CASBAH. STREETS. OUTSIDE.
MORNING.

*Women are clinging together after the beatings.*
*Someone is fleeing toward the terraces. We hear the deafen-ing whirl of the helicopters flying against the wind, their cabin doors open,* paras *sitting on both sides with their legs dangling out, their machine guns on their knees, a loudspeaker for every helicopter, microphones turned on in such a way that the din of the motors is multiplied a hundred times.*

*The helicopters fly low again, they skirt the terraces.*
*The Algerians are fleeing in terror, the uproar begins to fade*
*away, is less intense; microphones are turned on and off.*
*The terraces are emptied, men seized, beaten, dragged; all*
*the men are forced outside in the alleys, the streets, the*
*squares, every man is forced to face the wall, his hands up.*

SCENE 91

SHOPS. DOORS UNHINGED. OUTSIDE.
MORNING.

*A truck in reverse, a rope fastened to the hub of the wheels,*
*its other end to a door-latch. The motor is accelerated, clouds*
*of exhaust fumes . . .*
*Door latches pried open like lids of sardine cans, shop windows*
*smashed with machine-gun butts, the counters, the shelves,*
*flung into the air, the merchandise thrown into the streets; a*
*game, a frenzied excitement . . .*
*The Algerians watch, but can not intervene. Some shopkeepers*
*rush to the scene, crying despairingly, while others are dragged*
*away forcibly, tossed about, slapped, pushed, forced to open*
*their shops.*

SCENE 92

CANDY SHOP. INSIDE. MORNING.

*A shopkeeper is pushed behind the counter; he gets up, trem-*
*bling with fear.*
*A para asks him for a bag of candy, pays politely, smiles, pats*
*his bald head, and asks him sweetly:*

PARA: And the strike, my friend?

*Then he distributes the candy among the children who are*
*outside.*

# SCENE 93
CANDY SHOP. OUTSIDE. MORNING.

*The children take the candy silently, without thanking him, then eat the candies slowly, their faces unfriendly and cold . . .*

# SCENE 94
PLACE DU GOUVERNEMENT.
OUTSIDE. MORNING.

*The black sky, the trees, the advertising signs . . . Gordon Rouge . . . an equestrian statue, a car radio, a loudspeaker.*

LOUDSPEAKER: "Attention, people of the Casbah! The NLF wants to stop you from working. The NLF forces you to close your shops. Inhabitants of the Casbah, rebel against their orders. France is your country. France has given you civilization and prosperity: schools, streets, hospitals. People of the Casbah, show your love for your mother country, by disobeying the terrorists' orders. Algerians, return to work!"

*And then Algerian music, a cheerful and rhythmical melody; the Algerians are forced out of the Casbah in columns, and are pushed toward the military trucks which clutter the southern side of the square, and continue to arrive and depart.*

# SCENE 95
CASBAH. EXIT. OUTSIDE. MORNING.

*Meanwhile the* paras *of the psychological divisions make their first selection, randomly, or else deliberately, basing them on the slightest suspicions. They evaluate each man by his appearance or behavior. They block the Algerians from the exit ramp, and assault them with a battery of questions:*

PARA'S VOICES: Who are you? What's your name? Occupation? Where do you work? Why did you strike? . . .

They forced you, eh? . . . No . . . Tell the truth! You promised them, right? Then you're the one who wants to strike. Do you belong to the NLF? C'mon, answer me! Are you afraid to say it? Never mind, it doesn't matter.

*The Algerian does not answer, but stares into the* para's *eyes. The* para *turns to his companions and shouts:*

PARA: Jacques! . . . Jacques! . . . Another one to headquarters!

*The Algerian is seized, and pushed toward the truck.*

LOUDSPEAKER: "Attention, Algerians! The NLF wants to stop you from working. The NLF forces you to close your shops. The NLF wants to starve you and condemn you to misery. Algerians, return to work . . !"

SCENE 96

THE PORT. OUTSIDE. DAY.

*The port is deserted, the cranes still. A loaded ship sways lazily at her moorings, the fork-lifts are filled with supplies . . .*
*The limestone is dried out, the bridges empty, dangling cables swing slowly from the pulleys. There is silence in the docks . . .*
*Then the sound of motors approaching, clouds of dust, Arabs pushed out of the trucks, into the shipyard.*

SCENE 97

STREETS OF ALGIERS. OUTSIDE.
DAY.

*In the streets of the European city, there is an atmosphere of fear and doubt. The shop windows have their shutters lowered halfway, the shopkeepers are standing in the doorways, ready to close.*
*The front doors of houses are shut. There are a few hurried passersby but no automobiles; the trams are not running; on*

*the sidewalks the garbage is piled high, nearby the long brooms of the Algerian street cleaners.*

PARAS (*yelling*): *Sweep, mes enfants,* sweep.

*An Algerian with a very refined expression, a gentle appearance, says, while excusing himself:*

ALGERIAN: I don't know, sir, I'm sorry . . .

*They shove the broom into his hands, and shout to him:*

PARA: Learn!

LOUDSPEAKER: "French citizens! Europeans of Algiers! The strike called by the NLF is a failure. Do not be afraid. Return to your jobs. General Massu guarantees your safety. The Army will protect you!"

# SCENE 98

STREETS OF ALGIERS. OUTSIDE.
DAY.

*A jeep with loudspeaker precedes a row of military trucks loaded with Algerians.*
*In every truck there are two* paras *carrying machine guns by their sides. The Algerians are standing crowded together one against the other. Some of them are holding banners and signs:*
I AM GOING TO WORK BECAUSE I AM FREE.
WE ARE FREE.
ARMY-POPULATION-PEACE.
THE ARMY PROTECTS OUR RIGHTS.
*The trucks turn a corner, a youth jumps from the last truck, falls, gets up again, and breaks into a run.*
*The* paras *shout to him to stop, their voices mix with that of the loudspeaker.*
*The Algerian continues to run.*
*A burst of machine-gun fire, then another.*
*The Algerian jerks forward, his back curved, his arms raised. He falls down.*

COMMISSIONER'S OFFICE. PRESS
ROOM AND STAIRWAY. INSIDE. DAY.

*Noise, confusion in the Commissioner's office press room, ticking of the teletype machines, throngs of journalists in the telephone room. They are trying to transmit the first news.*
VARIED VOICES.
*Shouting in every language is heard.*

A JOURNALIST: We are now in the fourth day and the strike continues, with total support by the Arab population. The city is very calm. However—Calm . . . Are you deaf? The city is peaceful. In the Moslem quarters, in the outskirts of the city, in the Casbah . . . Bye, will call again, I'm busy.

*Through the open door, Mathieu can be seen passing, accompanied by another officer. Some journalists see him, and rush behind him. Some others follow, four or five in all, trying to stop him.*

JOURNALISTS: Colonel, colonel . . . Excuse me, colonel, a statement . . . We don't know anything . . . You promised us a press conference . . .

*Now there is a meeting with the Commissioner.*

FIRST JOURNALIST: Will you tell us what is happening?

MATHIEU: Nothing. Absolutely nothing. We are still weighing the situation.

*They move to the landing and begin to ascend the stairway that leads to the second floor. The journalists have difficulty keeping up with Mathieu.*

MATHIEU: Look around. I've put everything at your disposal. Go take a look with your own eyes.

2ND JOURNALIST: The strike is a success; but . . .

MATHIEU: No. It has failed in its objective.

1ST JOURNALIST: Insurrection?

MATHIEU: Insurrection.

2ND JOURNALIST: But the NLF has always spoken of a strike as a demonstration . . .

MATHIEU: And you believe the NLF?

2ND JOURNALIST: They seemed to be plausible this time. A general strike is a good argument for the UN.

MATHIEU: The UN is far away, dear sir. It is easier to make oneself heard with bombs. If I were in their place, I would use bombs.

1ST JOURNALIST: Armed insurrection . . . but what is it exactly?

OFFICER: It is an armed insurrection . . .

*They have arrived at the second-floor landing, hurry along, and stop in front of a large door, where there is a written sign:* PREFECT. *Mathieu, at the same time, has continued speaking.*

MATHIEU: It is an inevitable stage in revolutionary war; from terrorism, one passes to insurrection . . . as from open guerrilla warfare one passes to real war, the latter being the determining factor . . .

3RD JOURNALIST: Dien Bien Phu? . . .

MATHIEU: Exactly.

*Mathieu glances at the journalist, as if to see if there were any irony in his remark, but the journalist's face is expressionless.*

MATHIEU: In Indochina, *they* won.

3RD JOURNALIST: And here?

MATHIEU: It depends on you.

4TH JOURNALIST: On us? You aren't thinking of drafting us by any chance, are you, colonel?

*Mathieu leans his hand on the door handle and smiles at the journalists.*

MATHIEU: No! We have enough fighters. You have only to write, and well, if possible.

1ST JOURNALIST: What's the problem then?

MATHIEU: Political support. Sometimes it's there, sometimes not . . . sometimes, it's not enough. What were they saying in Paris yesterday?

5TH JOURNALIST: Nothing . . . Sartre has written another article . . .

*Mathieu gestures and makes an expression as if to say: "see what I mean?" At the same time, he opens the door. But before entering, he turns again to the journalists.*

MATHIEU: Will you kindly explain to me why all the Sartres are always born on the other side?

5TH JOURNALIST: Then you like Sartre, colonel . . .

MATHIEU: Not really, but he's even less appealing as an enemy.

# scene 100

PLACE DU GOUVERNEMENT AND
RUE DU DIVAN BLOCKADE.
OUTSIDE. SUNSET.

> *Place du Gouvernement, dusk, the other side of the blockade
> is silent, only the uncovered eyes of the Algerian women who
> await their men.*
> *The trucks continue to arrive: the men are forced to descend
> and allowed to enter the Casbah. There is an atmosphere of
> sadness, for not all the men have returned. The women look
> at them, scrutinize their faces, from the first to the last in
> one glance, then slowly . . . one face at a time. Some women
> recognize their husbands, or their brothers or their sons, and
> run to meet them . . .*
> *But others continue to ask for news in lowered, sorrowful
> voices.*

AD-LIB VOICES: Have you seen Mohamed? Where? When? Why
hasn't he returned?

> *A steady hum of voices in Arabic; then the monotonous voice
> of a policeman who speaks in the microphone of the loud-
> speaker.*

LOUDSPEAKER: "The NLF wants to stop you from working. The
NLF forces you to close your shops. Inhabitants of the Casbah, dis-
obey their orders. France has given you civilization and prosperity:
schools, streets, hospitals. People of the Casbah! Show your love
for your mother country by disobeying the terrorists' orders."

> *The loudspeaker is attached to one of the blockade posts, and
> from it a long wire for the microphone is hanging. The police-
> man has a raspy and bored voice; he stops speaking and leans
> the microphone on the table in front of him. He gets up, lights
> a cigarette, and moves away a few steps.*
> *Two children are among the women and behind the wooden
> horses barricades. They were waiting for this moment.*

*They bend, seem to be playing, but one of them lifts the barbed wire as high as he can from the ground. Petit Omar passes a wire underneath, its farthest end bent in the form of a hook. He moves it toward the microphone cord which is lying coiled on the ground. He succeeds in clasping it and pulls it toward him slowly. The cord unwinds, lengthens, stretches, until the microphone on the table begins to move, until it reaches the edge of the table, and falls . . .*

*The noise re-echoes in the loudspeaker, but no one pays any attention to it.*

*Petit Omar waits a second, then begins to pull again.*

*The microphone is dragged along the ground—a humming sound—it moves nearer, inch by inch, forward, under the barbed wire, until the children are able to take it, and disappear with it behind the women.*

LOUDSPEAKER: "Algerians! Brothers! Do not be afraid! Algeria will be free. Be courageous, brothers! Resist! Do not listen to what they are telling you . . . Algeria will be free . . ."

*The voice is not violent, but gentle, somewhat breathless and hurried. It extends to the whole square, so that all can hear it well: the people stop what they are doing to listen. They are emotional, proud, or angry, and look toward the sky where the voice seems to be diffused, as if those words should be written up above.*
*The officer is slow to realize what has happened, looks at the loudspeaker, the cord, and now grabs it, cursing.*
*He pulls and tugs it; the wire yields, and he wrenches it from the microphone.*

LOUDSPEAKER: "Brothers—"
*The voice is no longer heard, nothing more, silence.*
*Silence, only that something is changed in the women's eyes. The veils that cover the lower half of their faces suddenly begin to tremble, sway as if shaken by a breath, a light wind. There is no longer an atmosphere of sadness, or silence.*
JU-JU.
*The ju-jus attack the air, invade it, shake it, make it vibrate as if they were electric charges, or the sound produced by the wind on a field of dry reeds, or the sound produced by a hundred, a thousand fingernails that are scratching a window pane . . .*

SCENE **101**

HEADQUARTERS. PARA.
OUTSIDE. DAY.

PARA: One, two, three, four . . . Inside! C'mon!

*The five Algerians indicated are forced to get up, taken, pushed, and brought inside a large deserted house which is the* paras' *headquarters.*
*The other Algerians, about a hundred of them, are sitting on the ground, in the clearing in front of the house, and the*

paras *of the first regiment continue to guard them with pointed machine guns* . . .
*Suddenly from the villa, the music of a French song comes forth at full blast.*
*The Algerians look at each other nervously. Even a young para seems to be upset.*

1ST PARA (*turning to other* para): What are they doing?

2ND PARA (*smiling*): Dancing inside . . .

SCENE 102

HEADQUARTERS. VILLA.
INSIDE. DAY.

*A para rushes through a corridor carrying a tape recorder, enters a room where there are some sergeants and an Algerian.*
*The adjoining room with white tiled walls and a sink is visible through an open door. Two paras are sitting on the floor, smoking and chatting between themselves in whispers.*
*The para places the tape recorder on the table. The Algerian is naked to the waist. Signs of torture are visible. His face is swollen and wet. The sergeant places the chair near him, and helps him to sit down, then starts the tape recorder. He says to the Algerian who is trembling:*

SERGEANT: Go ahead! C'mon . . . Repeat everything from the beginning, and then we'll let you go. Name . . .

ALGERIAN: Sid Ahmed.

SERGEANT: Second name.

ALGERIAN: Sail.

SERGEANT: Which "district" do you belong to?

ALGERIAN: Second district . . .

SERGEANT: Second district . . . Explain better . . .

ALGERIAN: Second district, Casbah, West Algiers.

SERGEANT: What "group"?

ALGERIAN: Third group.

SERGEANT: Third group. What's your assignment?

ALGERIAN: Uh . . . responsible for the sixth section.

SCENE 103

VILLA. HEADQUARTERS.
INSIDE. DAY.

*In a room on the ground floor, a captain is bent over a large map with graphs, and is writing the name Sid Ahmed Sail in one of the blocks at the bottom of the pyramid . . .*

*At the same time,* paras *are seen through the large window, bringing other Algerians to the villa, and immediately afterward, the music and song are heard again very loudly.*

SCENE 104
CASBAH ALLEY. OUTSIDE.
NIGHT.

*Night, darkness, locked doors. The Casbah is silent. The* paras *tread noiselessly on their rubber soles. Patrols.*
*A flashlight searches for the number of a door, then stops. A* para *knocks discreetly.*
NOISES INSIDE. VOICES.

ALGERIAN VOICE: Who is it?

PARA: Sid Ahmed . . . Sid Ahmed Sail.

*The door is opened, the* paras *break in.*

SCENE 105
ANOTHER ALLEY. CASBAH.
OUTSIDE. NIGHT.

*Another alley in the Casbah, other* paras.
*Another door forced open, broken into.*
*Algerians are crowded together in a courtyard which is illuminated with electric flares.*
*They are being interrogated.*

SCENE 106
CASBAH STREET.
OUTSIDE. DAY. RAIN.

*A cloudy day, a light drizzle, a sloping street, Algerian music.*
*A company of zouaves walk two by two in the Casbah, through*

*the alleys, stop, play their music, and move on again, alter-*
*nating Algerian music and a French song.*
*Behind them, a line of donkeys with baskets full of packages*
*and bags, and cheerful* paras *who are joking, as they distrib-*
*ute the supplies to the starving women and children who stand*
*ashamed in front of their houses, their eyes lowered, their*
*gestures too brusque, and hesitant.*

SPEAKER: "At the General Assembly of the United Nations, none
of the motions presented in the course of the debate has obtained
the necessary majority. At last an agreement has been reached on
a resolution that excludes any form of direct intervention by the
UN in the Algerian question. The Assembly of the United Nations
has limited itself to expressing the hope that in a spirit of coopera-
tion, a peaceful, democratic, and just solution will be found, that
conforms to the principles of the United Nations Charter . . ."

*The monotony of the last words is drowned out and lost. It is*
*raining more heavily now. The water has begun to run*
*along the sloping alleys. The walls are gray, wet; the doors*
*of the cafes and shops are barred with signs nailed upon them.*
THIS SHOP HAS SUPPORTED THE NLF STRIKE. THE PREFECT
HAS ORDERED ITS CLOSING UNTIL FURTER INSTRUCTIONS.
*The band of zouaves has stopped again, and now they are*
*playing* La vie en rose.

SCENE 107

VILLA HEADQUARTERS.
INSIDE. DAWN.

*In some parts of the villa a gramophone is playing* La vie en
rose.
*In the room on the first floor, through the large window, the*
*whiteness of the dawn is visible. The desk is cluttered with*
*beer cans and thermos. Mathieu and other officers have their*
*eyes fixed on the graph, where the captain is marking other*
*small crosses at the bottom of the pyramid. The scene is mo-*
*tionless; their expressions are dull. Everyone seems to be in-*

*capable of movement, overcome by the dull apathy that always follows a sleepless night.*
*Until Mathieu breaks the stillness of the scene.*

MATHIEU: Good . . . Good work . . . Now we can all go to sleep.

*And moving together with the others, he continues.*

MATHIEU: The end of the strike doesn't change anything. The directives remain the same. Give your men the usual shifts. We must remain in the Casbah: twenty-four hours a day!

*He turns and points to the graph.*

MATHIEU: We must cling to it, and work fast!

*Then he turns to the officers and smiling, says in another tone of voice:*

MATHIEU: Have any of you ever had a tapeworm?

*The officers say "no" and laugh.*

MATHIEU: The tapeworm is a worm that can grow to infinity. There are thousands of segments. You can destroy all of them; but as long as the head remains, it reproduces itself immediately. It is the same thing with the NLF. The head is the General Staff, four persons. Until we are able to eliminate them, we must always start again from the beginning.

*While he is speaking, Mathieu takes his wallet from his back pocket, opens it, takes out four photos.*

MATHIEU: I found these in the police archives. They are old shots, but I made some close-ups. Ramel . . . Si Mourad . . . Kader . . . Ali la Pointe. We must print a thousand copies and distribute them to the men.

*Meanwhile, the photos are passed around.*
*They are photos taken from identification cards, or blown up from some group shots, figures somewhat blurred, faded, smiling, peaceful . . .*

SCENE **108**

NLF LEADERS' HIDING PLACE.
INSIDE. DAY.

> *In the dim light, the four faces are barely illuminated. The shadows tone down their expressions: Kader, Ali la Pointe, Ramel, Si Mourad. They are crowded into the hiding place, sitting on the floor, motionless, their eyes staring straight ahead, their breathing heavy. From outside, noises, voices that are fading in the distance. Silence.*
> *Then a discreet knock, a remark in Arabic.*
> *The four breathe deeply, look at each other, then smile a little.*
> *Ali unslips the beam which, placed through an iron ring, is holding shut the door of the hiding place. Using the soles of his feet, he pushes against the square of wall: the light enters violently. It is not electric light, but daylight.*

*Kader blinks his eyes to accustom them to the light, then goes out on all fours; after him, Ramel, and then the others. They leave the hiding place that Ali built in the wash-house on the terrace.*

SCENE**109**

COMPLEX OF KADER'S HOUSE.
OUTSIDE. DAY.

*All of them have machine guns. Ramel is very tall and robust, about thirty years old.*
*Si Mourad is slightly older than Ramel. His movements are slow and precise; his glance expresses patience and authority. Djamila is waiting for them.*

DJAMILA: You can come out. Thank God. There were so many this time, about ten.

*Ali recloses the hiding place.*

KADER: Paratroopers?

DJAMILA: Yes.

KADER: What do you think? Did they come here on purpose or by accident?

DJAMILA: No. By accident. They asked some questions, but they didn't touch anyone.

*Ali has come out of the wash-house. The sun is high, and helicopters are seen passing one another in the sky. On some far-away terraces, bivouacs of paras are visible. They are guarding the Casbah from above.*
*The rumble of motors and the voice of the loudspeaker are heard more clearly as they near the house.*

LOUDSPEAKER: "Attention! Attention! Inhabitants of the Casbah! The terrorist Ben Amin has been executed this morning. Qrara Normendine has been arrested. Boussalem Ali has been arrested. Bel Kasel Maussa has been arrested. Inhabitants of the Casbah! the NFL has been defeated. Rebel against the remaining terrorists who want to force you to continue a bloody and futile struggle. People of the Casbah, the terrorist Ben Amin has been executed. Help us to build a free and peaceful Algeria. Inhabitants of the Casbah, the NLF has been defeated. Rebel against the remaining terrorists who want to force you to continue a bloody and futile struggle. Attention! Attention! Inhabitants of the Casbah! The ter- rorist Ben Amin has been executed this morning. Qrara Normen- dine has been arrested. Boussalem Ali has been arrested. Bel Kasem Moussa has been arrested. Inhabitants of the Casbah—the NLF has been defeated . . ."

> *The voice fades away and is no longer heard.*
> *At the same time, a woman has come up from the floor below, carrying a tray of cups and a teapot.*
> *Ali looks at her quickly, but then watching her more closely, he sees that she is crying. When she passes near him, he stops her, places his hand kindly on her shoulder, and asks her in Arabic why she is crying.*
> DIALOGUE IN ARABIC BETWEEN ALI AND WOMAN.
> *The woman shakes her head, tries to smile, but says nothing. Then she enters the wash-house silently and begins to serve the tea.*

KADER: It's better to split up, to increase our chances. We must change hiding places, and change them continually . . . In the meantime, we must make new contacts, replace our arrested broth- ers, reorganize our sections—

ALI (*interrupting him*): Yes, but we must also show them that we still exist.

KADER: Of course. As soon as possible.

ALI: No, immediately. The people are demoralized. Leave this to me . . .

KADER: No. Not you, or any one of us. As long as we are free, the NLF continues to exist in the Casbah. If they manage to take us too, there won't be anything left . . . And from nothing comes nothing . . .

RAMEL (*intervening*): But it's also necessary to do something . . .

KADER: And we will do something, don't worry. As soon as we have reestablished contacts . . .

MOURAD: And our movements?

KADER: For this too we've got to change methods.

SCENE 110

MUNICIPAL STADIUM. OUTSIDE.
DAY. FEBRUARY 10, 1957.

*The municipal stadium is crowded with people. There is a football game between two European teams. It is almost the end of the first half. From above to the right of the guest box, there is a very loud explosion.*
*Strips of flesh are hurled into the air. Thick, white smoke . . . There are screams of terror. The people try to move away in haste. They are shoving, pushing, bumping into one another . . . Then calm returns. The sirens of the ambulances are heard.*
*The stretcher, the dead carried away, scores of wounded.*

SCENE 111

PREFECT'S OFFICE. PRESS HALL.
INSIDE. DAY. FEBRUARY 25.

*Ben M'Hidi is standing in front of the journalists with handcuffs on his wrists and ankles. He is without a tie. He is smiling a little, his glance ironical. There are two* paras *behind him with machine guns ready. The picture is still for an instant; Ben M'Hidi's smile is steady, so too his eyes, his entire face. Flashes, clicking of cameras.*

1ST JOURNALIST: Mr. Ben M'Hidi . . . Don't you think it is a bit cowardly to use your women's baskets and handbags to carry explosive devices that kill so many innocent people?

*Ben M'Hidi shrugs his shoulders in his usual manner and smiles a little.*

BEN M'HIDI: And doesn't it seem to you even more cowardly to drop napalm bombs on unarmed villages, so that there are a thousand times more innocent victims? Of course, if we had your airplanes it would be a lot easier for us. Give us your bombers, and you can have our baskets.

2ND JOURNALIST: Mr. Ben M'Hidi . . . in your opinion, has the NLF any chance to beat the French army?

BEN M'HIDI: In my opinion, the NLF has more chances of beating the French army than the French have to stop history.

*The press hall in the prefect's office is crowded with journalists of every nationality. At the side and central aisles there are photographers and cameramen.*

*Ben M'Hidi is opposite them, standing on a low wooden plat-form. Mathieu is next to him, seated behind a small desk. Mathieu now gets up, and signals to two paratroopers. Another journalist simultaneously has asked another question:*

3RD JOURNALIST: Mr. Ben M'Hidi, Colonel Mathieu has said that you have been arrested by accident, practically by mistake. In fact, it seems that the paratroopers were looking for someone much less important than yourself. Can you tell us why you were in that apartment at rue Debussy last night?

*The two paras have moved forward and they take Ben M'Hidi by the arms. At the same time, he answers.*

BEN M'HIDI: I can only tell you that it would have been better if I had never been there . . .

MATHIEU (*intervening*): That's enough, gentlemen. It's late, and we all have a lot of work . . .

*Ben M'Hidi glances at him ironically.*

BEN M'HIDI: Is the show already over?

MATHIEU (*smiling*): Yes, it's over . . . before it becomes self-defeating.

*The paras lead Ben M'Hidi away. He moves away with short steps, as much as he can with the irons that are tightened around his ankles. Mathieu has turned to the journalists and smiles again.*

SCENE 112

PREFECT'S OFFICE. PRESS HALL.
INSIDE. DAY. MARCH 4.

*Colonel Mathieu is standing. On his face is a brief smile, motionless, his eyes attentive, but half-closed somewhat, due to the camera flashes.*

1ST JOURNALIST: Colonel Mathieu . . . the spokesman for the residing minister, Mr. Gorlin, has stated that "Larbi Ben M'Hidi committed suicide in his own cell, hanging himself with pieces of his shirt, that he had used to make a rope, and then attached to the bars of his cell window." In a preceding statement, the same spokesman had specified that: ". . . due to the intention already expressed by the prisoner Ben M'Hidi to escape at the first opportunity, it has been necessary to keep his hands and feet bound continually." In your opinion, colonel, in such conditions, is a man capable of tearing his shirt, making a rope from it, and attaching it to a bar of the window to hang himself?

MATHIEU: You should address that question to the minister's spokesman. I'm not the one who made those statements . . . On my part, I will say that I had the opportunity to admire the moral strength, intelligence, and unwavering idealism demonstrated by Ben M'Hidi. For these reasons, although remembering the danger he represented, I do not hesitate to pay homage to his memory.

2ND JOURNALIST: Colonel Mathieu . . . Much has been said lately not only of the successes obtained by the paratroopers, but also of the methods that they have employed . . . Can you tell us something about this?

MATHIEU: The successes obtained are the results of those methods. One presupposes the other and vice versa.

3RD JOURNALIST: Excuse me, colonel. I have the impression that perhaps due to excessive prudence . . . my colleagues continue to ask the same allusive questions, to which you can only respond in an allusive manner. I think it would be better to call things by their right names; if one means torture, then one should call it torture.

MATHIEU: I understand. What's your question?

3RD JOURNALIST: The questions have already been asked. I would only like some precise answers, that's all . . .

MATHIEU: Let's try to be precise then. The word "torture" does not appear in our orders. We have always spoken of interrogation as the only valid method in a police operation directed against unknown enemies. As for the NLF, they request that their members, in the event of capture, should maintain silence for twenty-four hours, and then, they may talk. Thus, the organization has already

had the time necessary to render useless any information furnished
. . . What type of interrogation should we choose? . . . the one
the courts use for a crime of homicide which drags on for months?

3RD JOURNALIST: The law is often inconvenient, colonel . . .

MATHIEU: And those who explode bombs in public places, do they
perhaps respect the law? When you asked that question to Ben
M'Hidi, remember what he said? No, gentlemen, believe me, it is
a vicious circle. And we could discuss the problem for hours without reaching any conclusions. Because the problem does not lie
here. The problem is: the NLF wants us to leave Algeria and we
want to remain. Now, it seems to me that, despite varying shades
of opinion, you all agree that we must remain. When the rebellion
first began, there were not even shades of opinion. All the newspapers, even the left-wing ones wanted the rebellion suppressed.
And we were sent here for this very reason. And we are neither
madmen nor sadists, gentlemen. Those who call us fascists today,
forget the contribution that many of us made to the Resistance.
Those who call us Nazis, do not know that among us there are
survivors of Dachau and Buchenwald. We are soldiers and our
only duty is to win. Therefore, to be precise, I would now like to
ask you a question: Should France remain in Algeria? If you
answer "yes," then you must accept all the necessary consequences.

SCENE 113
CASBAH HOUSES. TORTURE
SEQUENCE. INSIDE. DAY.

*Casbah, bedrooms, kitchens, bathrooms.*
*Sharp, white light; motionless faces, figures paused midway*
*in gestures.*
*Women, children . . . glassy eyes . . .*
*Background motionless like in a landscape.*
*Algerians . . . wild eyes . . . animals being led to slaugh-*
*ter.*
*Paras, their every gesture measured exactly, perfection*
*achieved.*

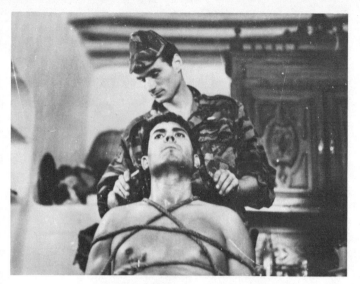

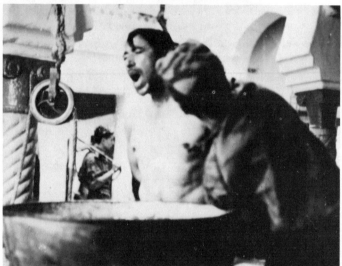

*An Algerian is lying down on the table, his arms and ankles bound with belts.*

*An Algerian, in the form of a wheel, an iron bar in the curvature of his knees, his ankles tied to his wrists.*

*Electrical wires wrenched from their outlets, a generator with crank, extended pliers with their prongs open wide, the tops of the wires held between two prongs, the pliers applied to a naked body, the most sensitive parts: lips, tongue, ears, nipples, heart, sexual organs . . .*

*Faucets, tubing, buckets, funnels, a mouth forced open, held open with a wooden wedge, tubing in the mouth, rags scattered around, water, a belly that is swelling . . . The torture is precise in every detail, and every detail points to a technique that is taken apart and reassembled.*

## SCENE 114
UPPER CASBAH ALLEY. OUTSIDE.
DAY.

*The chorus of the Koran school like ceaseless wailing, like a stubborn will to survive that seems to be spreading through the Casbah.*

*Petit Omar looks up instinctively, his small face hardened and taciturn, like that of an adult, then enters the school.*

## SCENE 115
KORAN SCHOOL. INSIDE. DAY.

*The children are sitting on the mats, motionless; only their lips are moving. There is an oblique light, the teacher is in the shadow.*

RELIGIOUS CHORUS.

*Petit Omar approaches the teacher who shakes his head in denial. Omar goes out.*

CASBAH STREETS. PATROLS.
OUTSIDE. DAY.

*The Casbah is patrolled by paratroopers; helmets, machine guns, portable radios, police dogs . . .*

*Paratroopers are erecting loudspeakers at every street corner. Paratroopers with brushes and buckets of paint are marking the doors of the Casbah with large numbers. From time to time, machine-gun fire is heard in the distance.*

*Algerians are standing against the wall, their hands up. There is a dead man a few feet away, an Algerian youth. The paratroopers turn him over and search him. A child with terrified eyes turns around a little.*

*A* para *transmits the dead man's name into the portable radio.*

# SCENE 117

CASBAH. OTHER STREETS.
OUTSIDE. DAY.

*A car radio receives and transmits the same name; and then the name is repeated by the loudspeakers scattered throughout the Casbah.*

LOUDSPEAKER: "Inhabitants of the Casbah! The rebellion gets weaker every day. The terrorist Ben Amin has been executed. Kasem Moussa has been arrested. He was commander of the 2nd Sector NLF. Inhabitants of the Casbah! The terrorists are not your true brothers. Leave them to their fate. Rely on the protection of the French army. Denounce the terrorists and agitators. Cooperate with us to reestablish peace and prosperity in Algeria . . ."

# SCENE 118

FOUR WOMEN. STREET.
OUTSIDE. DAY.

*Four women, their faces veiled, meet a patrol of* paras *in a small street.*

*Two of the* paras *stop the last woman, and lift her dress, uncovering her feet and ankles—those of a man. They tear away her veil.*

*The man is Ali. At the same time, there is . . .*

MACHINE-GUN FIRE.

*The two* paras *fall to the ground. Ali grasps his weapon, visible through the opening of his cloak.*
*The other* paras *fling themselves to the ground.*
*The other three women flee, while Ali continues to shoot, then runs away.*
*The four flee through the narrow streets and alleys, climb a stairway, and leap from one terrace to another.*
*Behind them, shouts, whistles, and machine-gun fire are heard. And moving nearer . . .*
BARKING OF DOGS.

## SCENE 119
COURTYARD WITH WELL.
OUTSIDE. DAY.

*The four enter a courtyard. Ali's three companions have also lifted their veils. They are Kader, Mourad, and Ramel.*
*A woman rushes to shut the door while a man leads the four toward an opening hidden by some boxes.*
*The others who are in the courtyard, women and children, are also busy helping, silently, hurriedly, in a tense atmosphere of solidarity with the four fugitives.*
*Very near are heard . . .*
BARKING OF DOGS AND PARAS' HURRIED FOOTSTEPS.
*A woman runs toward the door and throws some large hand-fuls of pepper under the cracks.*

## SCENE 120
STREET COURTYARD WITH WELL.
OUTSIDE. DAY.

*The group of pursuers—paras who are holding police dogs by leashes—slow down in front of the door.*
BARKING DOGS.
*The animals sniff the ground, then move on together with the paras.*

# SCENE 121

ARAB BATH. INSIDE. DAY.

*Petit Omar enters the large steamy room. He moves near the manager and hands him an envelope.*
*The manager slips it quickly under the counter.*

SPEAKER: "To all NLF militants! Reorganize! Replace your fallen and arrested brothers. Make new contacts! This is a grave moment. Resist brothers! The General Staff leaves you free to take any and all necessary offensives . . ."

# SCENE 122

CASBAH HOUSE. INSIDE. DAY.

*All the inhabitants of a house. The men are in a row on the balcony of the first floor, their hands crossed behind their heads, their backs to the wall, while paras guard them with pointed machine guns.*
*Two paratroopers lead an Algerian girl forward: she seems to be exhausted, and can barely walk, her eyes half-closed.*
*They stop in front of the first man and ask her:*

PARAS: Is this one?

SPEAKER: "Our hearts are breaking before such outrages, our houses invaded, our families massacred. Brothers, rebel! Bring terror to the European city!"

# SCENE 123

ALGERIAN STREETS. OUTSIDE.
EVENING.

*The European city, evening, houses are being lit. People have finished working. They are going to the bars, cinemas, or for walks, or crowding the bus stops . . .*

*The wail of a siren at full blast, an ambulance, driven at
frightening speed.*

*The people move aside, jump to the sidewalks. The cars
squeeze to the right, stop.*

*The ambulance door is opened, a corpse is thrown out, falls,
rolls into the street.*

*The people rush to it. It is a hospital attendant's in white uni-
form with a knife stuck in his throat.*

*The sound of the siren decreases in intensity; the ambulance
is by now far away.*

## SCENE 124

### AMBULANCE. OUTSIDE/INSIDE.
### EVENING.

*In the driver's cab, there are two Algerian boys. Their hair
is curly, their shirts old and torn. They are sweating; their
eyes wide open, staring.*

*The one who is driving barely reaches the height of the steer-
ing wheel. He clutches it desperately. The other has a machine gun. He makes a remark in Arabic shouting to be
heard above the siren.*

*The driver takes a hand off the steering wheel, places it on
the dashboard, and tries all the switches until he finds the
one for the headlights. The high beams.*

*The other, meanwhile, is now on his knees on the seat. He is
leaning out the open window to his waist, and he begins to
shoot.*

## SCENE 125

### ROUTE OF AMBULANCE. OUTSIDE.
### EVENING.

*The pictures succeed one another in a dizzy rhythm; surprise,
terror, someone falls.*

SHOTS. SIREN.

## SCENE 126

AMBULANCE. OUTSIDE/INSIDE.
EVENING.

> *There is no more ammunition. The machine gun is thrown in the back of the ambulance. The siren is still at full blast. The auto races ahead at terrifying speed. The two boys don't know any more what to do, where to go, and the one who is driving has his eyes almost closed, as if he were dizzy.*
> *They reach a square.*
> SIREN.
> *The other points ahead to the left.*

# SCENE 127
## BUS SHELTER. OUTSIDE.
## EVENING.

*The people are crowded in a bus shelter. The one who is driving doesn't understand or doesn't want to.*
*The other shouts to him again and again the same phrase, then flings himself on the steering wheel, and turns it in that direction.*
*The bus shelter is nearer and nearer.*
*The people are paralyzed. They have no time to move. They are run down, rammed into.*
*The ambulance crashes into a pillar.*
*On the ground, all about, the bodies of dead and wounded. The boys' bodies remain motionless, their foreheads resting on the smashed windshield.*
*But the sound of the siren does not stop, and is heard, mournful and full of anguish.*

# SCENE 128
## RAMEL'S HOUSE. IMPASSE ST.
## VINCENT DE PAUL. OUTSIDE/
## INSIDE. DAY. AUGUST 26.

*Impasse St. Vincent-de-Paul, noon. There are helicopters in the sky, and* paras *fill the alley.*
*Their faces are pale and tense, their eyes wide open, their hands clutch their machine guns. There is a strange silence. Then a movement at the back of the alley, a voice, a brief greeting. Mathieu has arrived and he is saying to an officer:*

MATHIEU: Now is not the time for heroes. Give me the megaphone.

*Mathieu takes the megaphone in his hands and approaches an open door. Through the doorway the inner courtyard of the house is visible where the corpses of four paras are strewn about.*

*Ramel and Si Mourad are on the first-floor balcony, lying in wait behind the railings, so they are able to watch the door, courtyard, and the stairway that leads from the balcony to the terrace.*
*On the terrace there are other* paras *who are facing the balcony. From time to time they release a burst of machine-gun fire.*
*The voice of Mathieu is heard over the loudspeaker.*

MATHIEU: Ramel . . . Si Mourad . . . use your heads. If you go on like this, I wouldn't want to be in your place when you are captured . . . Because you will be captured in the end, and you know it too. Surrender! If you do it immediately, I promise that you will not be harmed and you will have a fair trial. Can you hear me?

*Ramel and Si Mourad look at each other.*

MOURAD: Who is speaking?

MATHIEU: Mathieu. Colonel Mathieu.

MOURAD: We don't trust you, colonel. Come forward, show your-self.

*A moment of silence.*

MATHIEU: I don't trust you either. First stand up so I can see you, and keep your hands still and well in sight.

*Mourad hesitates an instant, glances at Ramel, then:*

MOURAD: Okay. But we want your promise for a fair trial in writ-ing. Give us a written statement, Mathieu, and then we'll surrender.

MATHIEU: How can I give you this statement?

MOURAD: We'll lower a basket from the window . . .

MATHIEU: Okay, I'll make the statement in writing . . .

*Mourad shows his companion the two large time-bombs that are on the floor in front of him. He takes one, begins to prepare it, and regulates the mechanism.*
*At the same time, he tells Ramel in Arabic to go find the basket.*

*Ramel crawls past the doors which are all closed, and asks for a basket.*
*A door opens and an old woman appears. She hands him a basket with its cord rolled up.*

MOURAD (*without turning around*): A newspaper too, or a piece of paper . . .

*Ramel brings him the basket and newspaper. Mourad has loaded the time-bomb mechanism, and the tic-toc sound is sharp and clear.*
*Now he has to move the second hand. Mourad's hands do not tremble, his glance is attentive, concentrating. Ramel watches him without saying a word; his fear is obvious.*
*Without moving, his eyes glued to the bomb dial:*

MOURAD (*loudly*): Are you ready, colonel?

MATHIEU: Yes . . . But let me first see you.

*Mourad moves one of the clock hands to precede the other one by a minute. Immediately afterward he places the flat and rectangular bomb in the bottom of the basket.*
*The basket seems to be empty. The piece of newspaper protects its bottom. Mourad tells Ramel to get up, and he too gets up. Their machine guns are lying on the ground. Meanwhile, Mourad has begun to count to himself silently, his lips moving: one, two, three, four . . .*
*From the terrace, the paras can see Ramel and Mourad standing up not very far away, their empty hands resting near the basket on the railing. A para shouts:*

PARA: We see them. You can come.

*Mourad begins to lower the basket very slowly.*

MOURAD (*counting*): 60, 59, 58, 57, 56, 55, 54, 53 . . .

*Mathieu enters the courtyard together with an officer and other paras. He looks up toward the balcony, smiles, and shows them a folded piece of paper.*

MATHIEU: Here it is . . . you know that when I give my word, I keep it . . .

*Mourad does not answer, but looks at Mathieu as if to calculate the distance and time, and slows down even more the basket's descent.*
*Mathieu moves forward a few steps, as if to go for the basket that is hanging on the other side of the courtyard, but suddenly he seems perplexed for a second, and then changes his mind. He turns to the nearest* para, *and gives him the note.*

MATHIEU: You go . . .

*Mourad's face has remained motionless. In his expression there is a shade of disappointment. He sees Mathieu retrace his steps toward the door, and is now surrounded by a group of paratroopers . . .*

MOURAD (*counting*): 25, 24, 23, 22, 21, 20, 19 . . .

*The basket has stopped moving two yards from the ground. In order to reach it, the* para *has to step over the corpses of his dead companions, his face hardens, he reaches the basket, and extending his arm, he throws in the note.*
*The basket does not move; the* para *looks up.*

PARA (*muttering*): Hurry up, black bastard!

*Mourad smiles at him, and mumbles something in Arabic, a phrase that he doesn't manage to finish, for now is heard—the explosion.*

SCENE **129**

RUE CATON 4. FATHIA'S HOUSE.
INSIDE. NIGHT. SEPTEMBER 24.

*Rue Caton number four. It is 11 p.m. A large, badly lit room is filled with paratroopers and one of them is now being carried away on a stretcher. Another three or four wounded are seated on the opposite side of the room and are waiting their turn to be carried away.*
*Two* paras *are by the door. They look out from time to time, and are attentive, ready, with machine guns clutched by their sides.*

*On the other side of the room opposite the door, the Algerians
who live in the house are standing against the wall.*
*Mathieu is in front of them, and he is asking a group of
women:*

MATHIEU: Which one of you is Fathia?

*A woman about forty years old raises her eyes toward him.*

MATHIEU: Is it you?

*The woman nods yes.*

MATHIEU: Go up the stairs, and tell Kader that if they don't surrender, we'll blow up everything . . . Do you understand?

*The woman again nods yes, and without waiting for more
words, she moves toward the door, taciturn, silent. Mathieu
follows her, he pushes past her.*

MATHIEU: Try to convince him, if you care about your house . . .
Wait a minute . . . Do you want to get killed?

*He leans out the door and says loudly:*

MATHIEU: Kader, look. Fathia is coming . . . I wouldn't shoot . . .

*Then he steps aside and lets the woman pass.*

MATHIEU: Go on . . .

*Outside the door, there is a small landing, then a steep stair-
way, and at the top, a corridor. Fathia climbs the stairs that
are cluttered with empty magazines, with cartridge boxes.
The walls are chipped from the shooting. The ceiling is paral-
lel to the stairway at the same inclination, for part of its
distance. But for the last few yards, it straightens out and
lowers to become horizontal.*
*The floor of the hiding place is open. Inside are Zohra and
Kader.*
*Fathia repeats to them in Arabic what Mathieu has said to
her.*
*Kader listens to her then answers, he too in Arabic. Then he
smiles.*

KADER: Okay. You can tell the colonel to blow up whatever he likes. Go on, now.

*Fathia goes down the stairs, and reenters the room.*

FATHIA (*to Mathieu*): He said that you can blow up whatever you like . . .

*She, then, rejoins the other women.*
*Mathieu seems to be tired, he has lost weight, he is nervous.*
*He turns to his men, and slowly as he gives the orders, the* paras *begin to move.*

MATHIEU: Return to where the others are. Prepare the plastic. It should be placed on the ceiling of the stairway under the hiding place . . . a long fuse rolled up . . . Take cover . . . keep shooting while you are working. Quickly! Clear the house . . . Bring them outside, then check the rooms again . . . Hurry up!

*Kader gives Zohra a box of matches. She goes to the back of the hiding place where there is a bundle of papers. She lights them, then returns near to Kader who is inspecting the magazine of his machine gun.*
*There are only two shots left. The other empty magazines are scattered around. Kader turns to Zohra, and starts to speak, but suddenly his words are blurred by the sound of shots.*
*Kader and Zohra have to step back a little, because the shells are flashing at the edge of the opening.*
*The shooting stops. From the stairway, one end of a long fuse is thrown into the corridor. The other end is inserted into a plastic charge fastened to the ceiling of the stairway, under the hiding place.*
*Kader and Zohra can see two or three yards in front of them, below, into the corridor, where the end of the fuse is glowing and burning.*
*Kader too has lost weight, his beard is long. He looks at the fuse, then at Zohra. A second passes in silence. Now Zohra too looks at him, and Kader says calmly in his usual voice:*

KADER: It doesn't do any good to die like this . . . it doesn't help anybody . . .

*He leans out from the hiding place.*

KADER (*shouting*): Mathieu! If you give your word that you won't touch any of the other people in the house, we'll come out.

## SCENE 130

MILITARY CAR. INSIDE. NIGHT.

*Inside a military automobile.*
*In the back seat, Mathieu is sitting next to Kader who is handcuffed.*
*Zohra is in the front seat, between the driver and a para who has in his hand a large regulation pistol. The interior is lighted by the headlights of a jeep which is following directly behind the auto a few yards. Silence. Mathieu looks hastily at Kader, who is staring straight in front of him, and appears to be sullen and downcast.*
*Then Mathieu speaks in a pleasant tone, as if in friendly conversation.*

MATHIEU: If you had let me blow you up, you would have disappointed me . . .

*Kader turns to him, and replies, trying to maintain his own voice at the same level of indifference:*

KADER: Why?

MATHIEU: For many months, I've had your photo on my desk together with a dozen or so reports on you . . . And naturally, I am under the illusion that I know you somewhat. You never seemed the type, Kader, inclined to performing useless actions.

*Kader doesn't answer right away, then speaks slowly as if expressing the results of his doubts, a new point of view . . .*

KADER: You seem to be very satisfied to have taken me alive . . .

MATHIEU: Of course I am.

KADER: That proves that I was wrong. Evidently I credited you with an advantage greater than I should have.

MATHIEU: No. Let's just say that you've given me the satisfaction to have guessed correctly. But from the technical point of view, it isn't possible to speak of advantages. By now the game is over. The NLF has been defeated.

*Zohra has turned around suddenly. She is crying and speaks hastily in Arabic, violently, harshly.*
*Mathieu doesn't understand, and turns to Kader to ask him politely, although with a bit of irony:*

MATHIEU: What is she saying?

KADER: She says that Ali is still in the Casbah.

SCENE 131
CROWDED BEACH. OUTSIDE. DAY.

*Ali la Pointe's glance is sullen, heavy, motionless. He moves his head slowly in such a way so that his glance also moves in a semicircle.*
*White beach, fine sand, transparent sea, bodies stretched out in the sun, golden skin of girls; girls in bikinis, sensual, smiling, young men with narrow hips, with muscles well cared for, cheerful youth, naturally happy, enviable.*
*The children are building sand castles near the water's edge; the beach is shaped like a half-moon with rocky reefs at both ends . . .*
*A September Sunday, warm and calm. Ali is leaning on the wall. He is wearing a white wool cloak. Only his eyes are visible . . . the eyes of a hungry tiger perched above a path, on the lookout for innocent prey. Eyes that now gleam, cruel eyes, tension dilating the pupils . . . Then again the calm, a gloomy calm, a gratifying tension. The place is right, and the victims couldn't be better ones.*
*Ali moves, leaves the wall, crosses the street to a large city sanitation truck, one of those metallic trucks with no visible openings.*
*A young Algerian is at the steering wheel, a street cleaner. He is leaning his thin face on the wheel. His hands are dirty, by now unwashable from years of work.*
*Ali has climbed into the cab. The truck is in motion and leaves.*

# SCENE 132

SANITATION TRUCK. INSIDE. DAY.

*The name of the street cleaner is Sadek. He seems frightened. He looks around, hesitates before speaking.*

SADEK: Then the beach is okay, Ali.

*Silence. Sadek looks at him again, waiting, but Ali does not respond.*
*Ali looks straight ahead at the street bathed in sunlight, the tar that seems to be liquid, the villas that surround Algiers, the lemon trees, the oleanders . . . Then he speaks, but without turning to Sadek. He speaks in a whisper, his eyes continually staring straight ahead.*

ALI: We need two more, the biggest ones.

SADEK: And the others?

ALI: The others . . . let's wait and see.

*Sadek remains silent for a while.*

SADEK: I've looked, Ali, even where I work. Nothing. The ones who have not been arrested have left Algiers and gone into the mountains . . . And the others don't want to hear any more about it . . . they're afraid . . .

*Ali doesn't answer him. Silence.*

ALI: Can't you go any faster?

SADEK: Yes, sure . . . here.

*Sadek puts the truck in third gear, accelerates the motor, then shifts back again into fourth gear. The truck increases its speed. The road is straight, the outskirts of Algiers are visible.*

SADEK: If we don't find any others . . . should we call it off?

*Ali turns suddenly to look at him but says nothing. Sadek can feel those eyes on him, and tries to justify himself.*

SADEK: We can't plant all of them by ourselves . . .

*Ali speaks to him in a dry and indifferent voice.*

ALI: You don't have to plant anything. You only have to carry them, that's all.

# SCENE 133
## RUE DES ABDERAMES. ALI'S HOUSE.
## OUTSIDE/INSIDE. NIGHT.

*Night. At number three rue des Abderames, on the first-floor balcony, the stove fires are glowing. The women are cooking outside on their stoves built from tin containers. They are cooking in front of the doors of their homes. The doorways are lit up.*

*Ali passes along the balcony, passes by Mahmoud and his wife who are speaking in whispers by themselves and leaning on the railing. It is a warm and starry night. Mahmoud says some more words to his wife, still speaking in whispers, tenderly. Then he follows Ali who has stopped in front of the door.*

# SCENE 134
## ALI'S ROOM. INSIDE. NIGHT.

*In the room, there is Petit Omar who is cutting out some pictures from a comic book.*

*As soon as he sees Ali at the door, he stops, closes his book, puts the scissors in his pocket. He seems to be embarrassed at being caught in his childish game.*

*In the center of the room, there is a dividing curtain, pulled halfway to the side. On the other side, Hassiba is typing.*

*Behind Hassiba, next to the bed, the hiding place is open.*

*Ali enters. He seems tired, sweating. He removes his cloak, tosses it on the chair, and puts his machine gun on the table.*

ALI (*turning to Petit Omar*): C'mon, hurry. Go to sleep. Tomorrow we four have a lot of work to do: Mahmoud, Hassiba, you and I.

*Mahmoud has remained motionless at the door. Hassiba has stopped typing and approaches them. Omar says nothing, but there is a satisfied look in his eyes. He can't help stretching out his hand to touch the machine gun.*
*Ali sits down at the table, moves the machine gun away from Omar, and continues to speak, still talking to Omar.*

ALI: Because we can't find anyone else, Sadek will bring us there in the truck. You get out first and plant the bomb where I tell you . . . then return here quickly. But be careful that no one is following you. Then Hassiba will get out, and after her, Mahmoud. Then I will plant the ones that are left. They'll know that we're still strong . . . you can be sure of that.

SCENE 135

ALI'S ROOM. INSIDE. DAWN.
OCTOBER 7, 1957.

*The room is badly lit by a small lamp which is on the other side of the curtain. There is a mattress on the table and Petit Omar is lying on top, asleep.*
*Ali is lying on a mattress on the ground, fully dressed, with his machine gun by his side. His eyes are open, and he is listening to the far-away sound of a motor. He looks at his watch, gets up, and goes to open the door. Outside there is the first gray light of dawn. The sound is heard more clearly and seems to be moving nearer.*
*Ali returns to Petit Omar, stays a minute looking at him, then shakes him roughly. The child gets up immediately. He is trembling, as if he had slept with taut nerves, and jumps down quickly from the table. His eyes are open, but he is still sleepy.*
*Ali smiles for a moment, and runs his fingers through Omar's hair.*

ALI: Omar, Omar. C'mon. wake up. Hurry, little one. Today you're going to see fireworks.

*The child also smiles and his face relaxes, then brightens up. At the same time, he extends his hand and pats Ali's side. Mahmoud enters the room from the balcony. He is carrying a tray with four cups of coffee.*

MAHMOUD: It's almost time, isn't it?

ALI: Yes.

*Then Ali turns to the curtain and calls:*

ALI: Hassiba . . .

HASSIBA: I'm ready.

*Ali sits down and puts on a pair of sneakers.*
*Petit Omar has finished dressing.*
*The curtain is drawn, Hassiba appears, already dressed.*

MAHMOUD: I heard the sound of a truck before . . .

ALI: Me too. But I don't think it was Sadek. Otherwise he'd be here by now.

*Hassiba is dressed in European clothes, a skirt and blouse. She nears the table and takes a cup of coffee.*

HASSIBA (*smiling*): How is your wife now?

*Mahmoud's face is expressionless. He shakes his head.*

MAHMOUD: So-so . . .

*Ali has finished putting on his shoes. He takes a cup of coffee. In the same moment, outside the door is heard:*
MACHINE-GUN FIRE.
*The four are startled.*

ALI (*shouting*): Inside! Inside! . . .

*Simultaneously, all of them move toward the hiding place. Mahmoud's wife appears at the door. Her face is despairing, but she moves carefully, quickly, precisely. She closes the door. She puts the coffee cups back on the tray, and hides everything in the sink.*

*She goes to the other side of the curtain. Ali is entering the hiding place. The other three are already inside. Ali pushes the movable piece of wall toward him, and the woman helps him.*

*Then she takes a can from the night table; it is full of plaster mixed with coal dust. The woman spreads the paste in the joints between the bricks of the wall and the closure of the hiding place. At the same time, shouting, shots, and the footsteps of paras are heard.*

*As soon as she has finished, the woman slips into bed under the sheets.*

*The paratroopers break into the room shouting, and make the woman get up. They drag her outside on the balcony.*

# SCENE 136

ABDERAMES COURTYARD. OUTSIDE.

DAWN.

*They drag Mahmoud's wife down from the balcony to the center of the courtyard, where now all the inhabitants of the building are standing—men, women, children—all of them with their hands to the wall, in full sight of the* paras *who are guarding them.*

*Sadek's head is lowered. He passes along the balcony between Mark and the captain. He stops in front of the door.*

CAPTAIN (*mumbling softly*): Here?

*The Algerian nods yes. They enter.*

# SCENE 137

ALI'S ROOM. INSIDE. DAWN.

*Sadek points toward the curtain. The captain signals him to go there. The Algerian points to a spot in the brick baseboard.*

*The captain examines it and with his thumb, he tests the fresh*

*plaster. He bends down and leans his ear to the wall. He
smiles as he listens to the . . .*

HEAVY BREATHING.

*It is the same breathing that soon after Mathieu hears, bent
in the same position as the captain. The colonel gets up and
looks around him.*

*Four* paras *are ready with their machine guns aimed at the
hiding place. Others are arranging plastic charges along the
wall, all of them connected to a single fuse.*

*In a corner, Sadek, wearing his cap and army camouflage fa-
tigues, is sitting on a chair.*

*He is watching the scene with his eyes wide open. He is trem-
bling. His body is slouched forward. He seems to be lifeless,
without nerves. If it weren't for his face, he would seem to
be a heap of rags.*

MATHIEU (*to the captain*): Everything ready?

CAPTAIN: Yes, sir.

MATHIEU: He hasn't answered?

CAPTAIN: No, sir. Total silence.

MATHIEU: I thought so. It was obvious.

*Mathieu bends down again and leans his ear against the bricks.
He gets up again. He remains a minute in this position, lost
in thought.*

MATHIEU (*loudly and markedly*): Ali . . . Ali la Pointe . . .
You're going to be blown up. Let the others come out, at least the
child. We'll let him off with reformatory school . . . Why do you
want to make him die?

*Mathieu stops, and shakes his head. He turns to the captain:*

MATHIEU: Let's go . . .

*A paratrooper is unrolling a large bundle of fuse.*

CAPTAIN: Bring it down there, till it reaches outside . . .

PARA: Yes, sir . . .

*Mathieu has stopped in front of Sadek. He looks at him.*

MATHIEU: Is this one still here? . . . Take him away.

*Two paratroopers grab the street cleaner by the armpits and almost lifting him completely, they lead him away. Mathieu is about to go out, then turns and takes the megaphone from the captain's hands, and places it to his mouth.*

MATHIEU: Ali! Ali la Pointe! I am giving you another thirty seconds. What do you hope to gain? You've lost anyway. Thirty seconds, Ali, starting now.

# SCENE 138

## ALI'S HIDING PLACE. INSIDE. DAWN.

*Ali la Pointe's eyes are staring at the square piece of wall that seals the hiding place. His glance is taciturn, gloomy.*
*The others are watching Ali. Their lips are half-open, their breasts rise and fall in laborious breathing.*

ALI (*in deep, resigned voice*): Who wants to leave?

*Petit Omar presses against Ali's arm; he looks like a son with his father.*
*Mahmoud takes his head in his hands and squeezes it.*

HASSIBA: What are you going to do?

ALI: I don't deal with them.

# SCENE 139

## ALI'S ROOM. INSIDE. DAWN.

*Mathieu checks his watch; thirty seconds have passed.*
*He moves to go out. The four paras with machine guns are still in the room.*

CAPTAIN (*to another paratrooper*): You stay here by the door to signal the others. When I call you, all of you come down . . .

SCENE 140
RUE DES ABDERAMES. OUTSIDE.
MORNING.

*The sun has risen to the height of the terraces.*
*The terraces are swarming with people.*
*The alley is empty and only the fuse is visible; it reaches to a
small clearing full of paratroopers. Two more colonels and a
general have arrived.*
*There is a paratrooper with an "Arriflex" ready to film the
explosion.*
*The atmosphere is that of a show. Two paratroopers are con-
necting the ends of the fuse to the electric contact.*

*On the terraces, there are Algerian women, children, and old people.*

*Their eyes are motionless; someone is praying. There is an atmosphere of suspense.*

*There is also the wife of Mahmoud; her eyes seem blank. Five* paras *come out of the house quickly, and pass along the alley toward the clearing.*

*The captain signals, and the* para *begins to lower the contact switch slowly.*

*The eyes of all are motionless. The camera is ready. But the explosion does not occur.*

*The paratrooper swears; he examines the wires.*

CAPTAIN: Stand back! Ready, Pierre?

*Pierre responds by mumbling something, and at the same time his hands are moving frenziedly around the wires.*

SCENE 141

ALI'S HIDING PLACE. INSIDE.
MORNING.

*Ali la Pointe bends over Petit Omar as if to cover him. Hassiba has stopped breathing, her eyes wide open; Mahmoud is crying . . .*
*A single image, a second and now:*
THE EXPLOSION.

SCENE 142

RUE DES ABDERAMES. OUTSIDE.
MORNING.

*The house collapses in a white cloud, as if its foundations had suddenly been removed.*
*Mathieu and the other officers move away. Behind them the echo of the explosion continues to resound, then shouts, orders, and isolated ju-ju.*
*Mathieu's face is weary but his expression is relieved. He is smiling.*

GENERAL: And so the tapeworm no longer has a head. Are you satisfied, Mathieu? In Algiers everything should be over.

MATHIEU: Yes, I believe there won't be any more talk of the NLF for some time.

GENERAL: Let's hope forever.

*Another colonel intervenes:*

1ST COLONEL: At heart they are good people. We've had good relations with them for a hundred and thirty years . . . I don't see why we shouldn't continue that way.

2ND COLONEL: Yes, but Algiers is not the only city in Algeria.

MATHIEU (*smiling*): Bah, for that matter, Algeria isn't the only country in the world . . .

GENERAL (*smiling*): Why, yes, of course . . . But for the moment, let's be satisfied with Algiers! In the mountains our work is always easier.

> *Gradually the officers move away down the slanting street toward their jeeps, and their remarks fade away and are lost.*

## SCENE 143

CASBAH STREETS. DEMONSTRATIONS.
OUTSIDE. DAY. DECEMBER 1960.

> *Like the cries of birds, of thousands of wild birds, the ju-jus invade and shake the black sky.*
> JU-JU-JU . . .
> *And below, in the Casbah the white cloaks of the Algerians are like streams, floods; through the alleys, down the stairways, through the streets and the squares, they flow toward the European city.*

## SCENE 144

PRESS HALL. PREFECT'S OFFICE.
INSIDE. DAY.

> *In the press hall, the journalists are taking the telephones by force, shouting at the top of their voices.*
> *An English journalist:*

JOURNALIST: No one knows what could have been the pretext. The fact is that they seem to be unleashed without warning . . . I telephoned Lausanne . . . yes, Lausanne. I spoke with an NLF leader in exile. They don't know anything there.

SCENE 145

ALGIERS STREETS. DEMONSTRATION.
OUTSIDE. DAY/NIGHT.

*In front, the adolescents, very young boys and girls, their mouths wide open, their eyes burning, laughing, their arms stretched above them, raised and lowered to mark the rhythm.*

VOICES: Algerie!
Mu-sul-mane!
Algerie Musulmane!

*The paratroopers jump down from the trucks, and rush forward.*
*The policemen rush forward, soldiers, zouaves, the CRS . . .*
*Deployed in cordons, in a wedge, in turtle-like formations, in order to divide, to scatter, to hold back . . .*
*But the demonstrators will not move back, or divide. They continue to press forward, pushing against the troops, face to face.*

VOICES: Free Ben-Bel-la!
Free Ben-Bel-la!

*The Europeans are closing their doors, lowering shutters. They too, the younger ones, the more decisive, are grouping together, trying to confront the Algerians. They are less numerous, but armed . . .*
*The first revolver shots resound in the streets, from the windows. Some Algerians fall, but the others continue to advance. They are running now, scattering.*

VOICES: Ta-hia Et-thou-ar! *

* Long live the partisans!

*The jeeps, the trucks, the sirens, the tear-gas bombs, machine-gun fire.*
*And then the tanks. The turrets move slowly in a semi-circle. The machine gunner fires the first burst at point-blank.*

VOICES: Ta-hia el-Djez-air!
Ta-hia el-Djez-air!

*Meanwhile the sun has set, and shadows of night are visible.*

VOICE OF ENGLISH JOURNALIST (*off*): Today the situation is tenser. In spite of pressure from the more intolerant colonialist group . . . it seems that the Government has given strict orders not to use arms except in emergency situations. But this afternoon there were attempts to enter the European city by force: as a result, the first casualties . . . Now calm has returned, although from the Casbah continue to be heard those cries . . . incoherent, rhythmic, nightmarish cries . . .

*And then, from time to time, in the by now dark night, the shrill and angry ju-jus.*
JU-JU-JU . . .

# SCENE 146

ALGERIAN STREETS. FLAGS.
OUTSIDE. DAY.

*Those cries continued until the following day.*
*The following day is sunny; the scene begins again like the day before. Only that . . .*

VOICE OF ENGLISH JOURNALIST (*off*): This morning for the first time, the people appeared with their flags—green and white with half moon and star. Thousands of flags. They must have sewn them overnight. Flags so to speak. Many are strips of sheets, shirts, ribbons, rags . . . but anyway they are flags.

*Thousands of flags. All are carrying flags, tied to poles or sticks, or waving in their hands like handkerchiefs. Waving in the sullen faces of the paratroopers, on the black helmets of the soldiers.*

SPEAKER: "Another two years had to pass and infinite losses on both sides; and then July 2, 1962 independence was obtained—the Algerian Nation was born."

VOICES: *Ta-hia el-Djez-air!*
Ta-hia el-Djez-air!
Ta-hia el-Djez-air!

*THE END*

# Gillo Pontecorvo

Director Pontecorvo lives with his wife and their two young boys in a small comfortable apartment on the top floor of a nine-story building near the Via Nomentana in Rome. It is an area known as The African Quarter. "The Fascists built it," he says, "for the veterans of *our* colonial misadventures."

His study is crammed with books, papers, antiques, bric-a-brac. Plants that he himself lovingly cultivates—prunes, divides, crossbreeds—are everywhere. Together with music they are this director's true passion. Stuck in the frame of a painting is a photograph of the *real* Ali la Pointe; in the corner of another is a snapshot of Pontecorvo with Picasso. "I interviewed him many years ago when I was a journalist," he explains. Sipping *grappa* we begin an easy flow of conversation touching on a million different topics—politics, art, skin diving, music, women, even backaches. We come to his current project, political of course: "I am attempting to portray a Christ who is the son of his times, times of crisis just like ours; a Christ who expresses the contradictions of an interim age. You see it is the story of a revolutionary in spite of himself. Jesus thought he was only moving on a religious level while his preaching was a sword striking at all levels of the oppressive and repressive Palestinian society that was dependent on the Roman *colonial* power." His voice with its never lost Pisan accent is soft, mellifluous, captivating. The eyes are large, laughing, sea blue—extraordinarily beautiful. The face is strong, bronzed, noble. His gestures, his talent for mimicry and inventing nonsense stories, his laughter, his enthusiasm—everything about him is young. I later discover that this witty, irreverent and altogether brilliant kid is in reality approaching his fifty-third birthday.

Gillo (Gilberto) Pontecorvo was born in Pisa, November 1919, of a family of Jewish origin. At eighteen, pursuing his passion for music, he started studying composition with René Leibowitz but had to give it up a few months later for economic reasons. He then enrolled in the university with the intention of concentrating on chemistry but was soon sidetracked by lengthy clandestine political discussions with anti-Fascist students and professors. It didn't take long for him to realize that his interest really lay in politics, and, after dropping out of school, he headed for France where, in Toulon, he acted as a liaison between underground groups in Italy and Italian exiles in France. By competing in international tennis matches he was free to travel abroad frequently without raising much suspicion. In 1941 he became a member of the Italian Communist Party and continued his political work in Italy. When the struggle against Nazi-Fascism erupted, he was a commander of the Resistance movement in Milan and the Alps, using the *maquis* name of Barnaba. Following the war he was a functionary of the Italian Communist Party. He then returned to France as a photojournalist in Paris for Agence Havas (now Agence France-Presse) but soon drifted into movie making as an assistant to Joris Ivens and Yves Allegret. His first award-winning documentaries in the early fifties established him as a director whose focus was man fighting against nature or social oppression. "I've always wanted to look at man during the hardest moments of his life." In 1956 he quit the Party to become a left-wing independent.

Though certainly one of the leading directors at work today, Gillo Pontecorvo has not been affected by fame or success, nor has he adopted the mental attitude and distorted psychology rampant among the movie community. He is unpretentious, has not become a "celebrity" surrounded by a court, does not own a Ferrari, shuns the cinema milieu. He would not give up his personal freedom for anything and only makes a movie when he is deeply convinced that it *should* be made. Arriving at that conviction takes him an average of four years. "The problem is to find a story you really believe in, a story you really love. Otherwise. . . ." The result: in eighteen years he has made only four full-length movies. He would not have wanted to direct more. The following interview took place in May 1972.
P.N.S.

# Gillo Pontecorvo's Filmography

| | | |
|---|---|---|
| Missione Timiriazev | (*The Timiriazev Mission*) | 1953-Short |
| Porta Portese | (*The Portese Gate*) | 1954-Short |
| Uomini del Marmo | (*Man and Marble*) | 1955-Short |
| Giovanna | | 1955 * |
| Pane e Zolfo | (*Bread and Sulphur*) | 1959-Short |
| La Lunga Strada Azzurra | (*The Long Blue Road*) | 1957 |
| Kapo | | 1960 |
| La Battaglia di Algeri | (*The Battle of Algiers*) | 1966 |
| Queimada | (*Burn!*) | 1969 |

* Italian episode of Joris Ivens' *Die Windrose* (The Compass Rose). Other episodes were directed by J. Ivens, A. Cavalcanti, A. Viany, S. Gerasimov, Y. Bellon, Vuo Kuo Yin.

# The Interview

*Interviewer:* What led you to make *The Battle of Algiers?*

*Pontecorvo:* I'll have to start off by explaining how *The Battle of Algiers* was the outgrowth of another project. After my second film, *Kapo*, colonialism was one of the themes I was most anxious to explore. At that time the Algerian situation had really brought colonialism to the fore; its revolution had touched, enraged, upset us, asserted itself so strongly that it became the catalyst for my next undertaking. So Franco Solinas and I began work on a film whose title was to be *Para.** We started out with the idea of depicting colonialism through the eyes of one man, a Frenchman, an ex-*para*. This fellow was the perfect product of industrialized Europe

* French abbreviation for paratrooper.

—handsome, articulate polished. But like the society he represented, he was hollow, empty, with only one overriding concern—
efficiency. He would be working as a journalist visiting colonial
countries. Eventually we got a script together but for a number of
reasons nothing came of it. I think some of these reasons were political—the producer probably wasn't terribly willing to get in bad
with the French. Then two years later, in 1964, Yacef Saadi, who
had been the military head of the National Liberation Front in the
Autonomous Zone of Algiers and plays the same part in *The Battle
of Algiers*, came to Italy looking for a director to make a movie on
the Algerian struggle. He had three names in mind: Luchino Visconti, Francesco Rosi, and myself. He couldn't reach an agreement
with Visconti, and Rosi was shooting *The Moment of Truth*. When
we talked about it I suggested using the *Para* script we had de-
veloped, believing it to be the best way of dealing with the relationship between colonizer and colonized. However Saadi felt that
*Para* treated colonialism too generally and didn't concentrate
enough on the Algerian situation. We finally agreed to make a
different film emphasizing one moment of their struggle on the
condition that I be completely free in handling the project my own
way.

*Interviewer:* Why did you choose as that moment the period of the
battle of Algiers?

*Pontecorvo:* We decided it together, as for them it was perhaps *the*
most important moment.

*Interviewer:* I'll put it this way. Why focus on a failure of the
liberation struggle as indeed the battle of Algiers had been?

*Pontecorvo:* To begin with you make a film in a flourish of excitement. If you don't feel literally turned on by your theme then the
film won't raise any enthusiasm from an audience. Now for me—
someone who approaches man and the human condition with a feeling of warmth and compassion—the most touching, fascinating,
and illuminating moment of the Algerian war, *what really turned
me on,* was the birth, development, and crumbling of the NLF organization in Algiers, in effect, the battle of Algiers. There were
moments during this battle, the general strike for instance, when
a concerted popular effort was necessary and these instances of-

fered me the possibility of recounting what I am most interested in: the feelings and the emotions shared by a multitude, the ability of the mass, in special moments, to express certain qualities and a kind of enthusiasm which you generally don't find in the individual. I was so compelled by suffering and strife on both sides, by the hope and the collective feelings set in motion by the events, that I wanted to make a film whose title could have been *Thou Shalt Deliver in Pain.* It was like filming the birth of a nation. We thought that that title was too unwieldy so we decided on *The Battle of Algiers* as the event was already well known in Europe.

*Interviewer:* What was the idea which inspired the movie?

*Pontecorvo:* In times like these when so many countries are still grappling with the problems of the struggle for independence and freedom we thought it both stimulating and important to focus not only on the techniques of urban guerrilla warfare and partisan war but also on how, with the right timing, a people or an ethnic group need simply set its mind on independence in order to begin an irreversible process which will eventually achieve that goal despite momentary defeats and setbacks. Even though some rivers seem to disappear, they run underground instead and always reach the sea. In the same way *The Battle of Algiers* shows the defeat of the NLF; then after two years of silence—the leaders dead or exiled, the organization destroyed—just when everything seems over for good, the movement explosively sets itself in motion again, thereby proving that nothing is lost on revolutionary ground because what has been sown springs up multiplied a thousand fold. I even tried to emphasize this irreversibility through visual means —the type of sequences we find at the end of the movie suggest this idea of the river moving again. The music also reiterates this concept. In terms of the score, *The Battle of Algiers* has an open finale. By suspending the final note I tried to place the poetic stress on development, on what has yet to happen and unavoidably will happen. If these ideas emerge, if the movie gives hope to all those people facing the same task, then the film has succeeded in its aim. Rather than showing the ferocity and the brutality of the repressive forces—as some extreme leftists would have had us do—it seemed more valid to place the importance on the fact that when a revolutionary situation is well timed and historically ripe the movement will keep on, nothing will be able to stop it, no matter what blows the organization which originally propelled it may receive. About the repressive forces, we tried to present the paratroopers as normal—not maniacs, sadists, or exceptional cases, let's call them products of rational, supercivilized France—because we meant our condemnation to reach beyond them to the political machine itself. In effect it becomes a historical condemnation of those men behind the *paras*—of colonialism itself. This seemed the more mature, purposeful thing to do instead of limiting ourselves to showing the *paras* with flaring nostrils, foaming at the mouth. To sum up, I am deeply convinced that there are processes in history which once begun cannot be stopped. Not only did we believe this to be right, but we really liked the idea that it was right. The world moves in a certain way. Remember how Ben M'Hidi answers the journalist who asks him whether the NLF has any chances left: "In my opinion the NLF has more chances of beating the French Army than the French have of stopping history." Bear in mind that the press conference is taking place during the *downfall* of the NLF in Algiers.

*Interviewer:* Why did you declare right after the movie was released, "My film does not intend to be anti-French"?

*Pontecorvo:* First, because I think it should have been made by a Frenchman and second because it is obvious that not all French agreed with the politics of their government in Algeria at that time. So why should it be anti-French? The movie was anti-colonial in general and anti the French permanence in Algeria in particular.

*Interviewer:* Why did you make *The Battle of Algiers* in black and white?

*Pontecorvo:* Although I don't want to theorize about this, I generally like black and white better. I feel that it gives me a broader range of possibilities in transposing my material than does color. However in *The Battle of Algiers* black and white was an absolute necessity of expression. First of all we had eliminated most of the so-called "indispensable" ingredients for a movie, like professional actors, or individual protagonists with their own personal stories. Instead, perhaps for the first time in cinema-fiction, we wanted the audience to identify with a *choral* protagonist—with the hope, the pain, the joy of an entire people. It was also one of the first, if not the very first European political film. Consequently we had to invent a new langua,e; we wanted to shoot under "the dictatorship of truth" avoidi.ig usual, easy, "profitable" cinematic effects lest they divert us from our goal. All of this called for a means of recounting which included a certain type of dialogue, music, acting, and editing, but most importantly a very special kind of photography—the photography through which people are most commonly accustomed to coming in touch with reality. Since the people are used to coming in contact with the black and white reality of the mass media—telephotos, TV newsreels, etc.—an image seems most true to them when it resembles those furnished by the media, those which inform him about what is happening in Vietnam, China, or on the moon. People practically never experience the great events of history with their own eyes—technically speaking you could say that the human eye is like a 32mm focal lens while the mass media audience is accustomed to seeing through the 200mm or 300mm lens. So not only did I want to shoot in black and white, I also wanted to use the same lenses which would reproduce images like those of the mass media.

*Interviewer:* Here you talk about *The Battle of Algiers* in terms of cinema-fiction. Once you told a journalist, *"La Bataille d'Alger est un film de fiction."* Now, wouldn't you say that shooting under "the dictatorship of truth" with its complete adherence to reality is just the opposite?

*Pontecorvo:* I called it that only to polemicize with those few who improperly called it a documentary. It's clear that the movie has a dramatic structure which has nothing to do with the documentary genre. Anyway, if it *must* be labeled let's just say it is a film with a collective protagonist.

*Interviewer:* I know you worked in photography before you started directing. I think this background shows in your work as a great deal of your directorial attention is on photography. This is especially true in *The Battle of Algiers.* . . .

*Pontecorvo:* You're right. I think I am one of the directors most interested in the photographic aspect of the image. For me the photography in a film is almost as important as music, dialogue—I

guess I can even say the story itself. I just can't believe that some
directors would allow the images they invent to be realized by the
cinematographer alone. Would a fellow who wants to write poetry
write down his ideas in prose and then give them to somebody else
to versify for him? Or would a composer write just the melodic
line of a piece and let someone else take care of the orchestration
and the instrumentation? Maybe I should clarify one thing before
I go any further. There is a tremendous difference between shooting indoors and out. The cinematographer has to have the last
word where interiors are concerned because of the kind of skill
it involves. No matter how knowledgeable a director may be about
photography, very rarely does he master the skill of indoor shooting. For example, when we are shooting interiors, if I realize that
the lights are wrong, I couldn't even begin to tell the cinematographer how to change them. I could only tell him that I want a
lighter or darker background, something of that sort. I couldn't
tell him how to get it; I couldn't possibly say, "Use a 10,000 watt"
or whatever. But exteriors are a completely different matter when
the director is keen on photography. Why? Because in exteriors
great effects can usually be attributed to the way colors appear in
certain conditions, the way for example drab, lead-colored weather
can effect greens and pinks. A director who loves the image and
believes it to be the language through which his ideas are realized
is willing to sacrifice other parts of the movie for the sake of
shooting at a certain hour of the day if he knows that only at that
hour will he find a pink hitting a tree in a particular way or a
splash of gray or a peculiar shade of green. He'll do things like
steal time from rehearsals or fight with the producers until conditions are what he wants. When the effects are good, you know,
when the critics (who are generally almost as ignorant about photography as the directors themselves) rave "What magnificent
photography!" it is seen as miraculous skill on the part of the cinematographer. Actually these "near miracles" are often due to the
director's choice of timing natural light, or deciding a moment
for shooting, or of camera angles, taste in colors, direction of light.
. . . Now let me bring up another point about photography. Where
cinema is at its dawn, where it needs to take giant steps forward, is
in exploiting photography more creatively. I think there is an enormous disproportion between innovations made by photographers

in still photography and those searched for in cinema photography. If you leaf through a catalogue of stills by several photographers or if you go see a photo exhibition you will note experiments, some obviously more successful than others, in very many directions. Go see a movie; it is very unusual to find any radical innovations in the photography. It may or may not be beautiful, but it is never really creative because any variations made are within the limited range of an "objective" representation of reality rather than a "transposition" of reality. In *The Battle of Algiers* I went ahead, just a tiny step ahead, beyond the usual passive photography. Still even that small step was fruitful, confirming my belief that there is much to be got from photographic innovations in the movies. In fact, I am convinced that part of the film's worldwide success was due to the kind of photography we used.

*Interviewer:* In your opinion why is it that more experiments aren't made to find different kinds of cinema photography?

*Pontecorvo:* Mostly because if you choose a style that is not the usual "objective" one it would be extremely difficult to maintain the photographic continuity throughout the film. Then, experiments take a great deal of time during the shooting; it could also be that directors don't search for innovations because they have a very easy, almost lazy attitude toward the language of their work. And cinema photography does not easily lend itself to experimentation because it is not the banks, the producers, or self-censorship that pose the strongest limitation but paradoxically the dictatorship of the lens. The possibility of "transposition" in the field of the image is severely limited because of the fact that we must work through a lens which compels us to adhere to reality and makes it extremely difficult to transcend it. In my next movie on Christ for instance there are some vision sequences where I'd love to be able to enjoy the marvelous freedom of a painter instead of being a director tied to the despotism of the lens. I hope I'll be able to avoid a few obstacles by playing on an abnormal use of light for the dream sequences of the movie—the Jungian part. I am trying to find a kind of grainy photography with very bright surfaces where faded whites devour the edges of the images—something close to the *pointilliste* style, like a Seurat emptied of colors and flooded with light. Without exaggeration let me say again that our main enemy in this area is the lens which only grants you crumbs of the freedom you must have to express yourself fully and grants even those crumbs only after an unfair, unbalanced struggle.

*Interviewer:* Marcello Gatti is your regular cinematographer. How important is he in your work?

*Pontecorvo:* As I said, his importance is decisive in the interiors. Inevitably when the cinematographer knows his job, and Marcello Gatti knows his extremely well, it weighs radically on the final result of the image. But sometimes I wonder if this is a positive fact, because ultimately I believe that a film, like any other form of artistic expression, should reflect the defects and the qualities of one specific person—the director. But even though I say this I have to add that I truly welcome the collaboration of people like Marcello Gatti.

*Interviewer:* Technically, how did you achieve the graininess in the photography with *The Battle of Algiers?*

*Pontecorvo:* For about a month before shooting I did phototests with my own camera and a 16mm. Then together with Marcello Gatti we made more tests with a 35mm camera. What we were searching for was a kind of photography that could be acceptable on a formal level—which is to say visually pleasing—but at the same time would contain the rough quality of a newsreel. We had begun experimenting, looking for this effect during the filming of *Kapo.* No matter how many discussions I had with the Yugoslavian cinematographer on the film he wouldn't come up with what I wanted. Seeing the dailies I knew that *Kapo*'s photography just wasn't right and by the end of the filming we were left with a negative that didn't work. I then went into the lab with Marcello Gatti, the second cameraman at that time, and some technicians determined to give the negative a rougher quality. We tried a process of duplicating the positive and that gave us some results. But because the negatives had not been prepared for this treatment some of the areas showed too strong a contrast. In *The Battle of Algiers* we used a number of ways to achieve that rougher quality and one of them was carrying ahead that duplication which we had first tried with *Kapo.* This time however, knowing we would be employing the process in the lab, we compensated for the sharp contrast by shooting everything extra smoothly. As a result we achieved the required grainy effect without any violent contrast. Another device we employed had to do with the way I shot the exteriors. It seemed to me that shade, diffused light, was much more dramatic. So all the exteriors—and the movie is practically all exteriors—were shot without the sun—in Africa!! What we did was cover the areas that were to be shot with forty- to fifty-yard sheets. And I wouldn't have shot outside if I hadn't been able to have at least some naturally shaded areas as well. But, by the same token, the photography had to have some guts, and since I knew more or less what the editing was going to be, I tried to have one very strong slice of light—even a very little slice—in a less important part, the corner let's say, of every three or four frames. This would give it some violence while at the same time retaining its general sense of smoothness. Of course when we were shooting in the Casbah's small streets it was easier to achieve these effects; in the large squares, on the other hand, I would stall, waiting to shoot with the kind of light I wanted, by conducting rehearsals until the sun settled behind a building.

*Interviewer:* How many cameras did you use?

*Pontecorvo:* Almost always one. You control the scene better. Sometimes in the crowd scenes we would use two, one zoom and the other hand-held by Marcello Gatti or myself. Of course for the explosions we had to use as many as ten cameras. Even though the houses were made of styrofoam we didn't have enough money to rebuild and re-explode them. Since we were only shooting once we had to make sure we would have enough editing material.

*Interviewer:* Do you often use a hand-held camera?

*Pontecorvo:* Well, I like using it very much. It allows you to follow an actor's movement and expression. If he is doing well in a given moment you can pull in close to him, adjusting on the spot. Or if you don't like what he is doing you can move back and away from him. I even rehearse scenes following them through the camera or the viewfinder. If I am not holding the camera I just can't visualize the scene well, while when I do hold the camera, I see it just as it will appear on the screen. And I am convinced that gestures do assume different meanings when they are framed by the viewfinder rather than seen with the eye's complete field of vision. The viewfinder allows you to evaluate within a context of volumes as though it were the frame, the finished product. So when I work with the actors I do hold the camera, choosing from reality what I want and ignoring the rest—it's like wearing glasses. You know the attitude is habit forming; it ends up permeating your private life as well. My wife and children tease me all the time because when we go for walks, look at landscapes, or even try to find the right spot at home for placing an armchair I'll bring my hands close to my eye and erase what I don't like.

*Interviewer:* What camera do you use?

*Pontecorvo:* The Arriflex which is light and easy to move.

*Interviewer:* How many meters of film did you shoot for *The Battle of Algiers?*

*Pontecorvo:* I don't remember exactly. About eighty thousand.

*Interviewer:* Did you record live?

*Pontecorvo:* Only the shouting and the screaming.

*Interviewer:* The French shot a lot of film during the Algerian war, I guess you saw it. . . .

*Pontecorvo:* Sure. It was quite useful.

*Interviewer:* But as the note in the beginning of the film says, you didn't use any of it.

*Pontecorvo:* Not an inch. Just for the record I should say that the caption was generously suggested by some American colleagues. We hadn't thought of putting it in. After seeing the film they said, "You mean there's no newsreel." "No, really," I told them, "I swear it on my children." "Well then," they replied, "you'd better put a note in at the beginning saying so, otherwise nobody is going to believe you." In fact the only ones who actually did believe it, who knew for sure that there was no newsreel in the film, were the French military who could tell that the guns in the movie were different from the ones they had been equipped with and that the tanks used were those bought by the Algerian government from Czechoslovakia *after* the liberation.

*Interviewer:* Why not use newsreel?

*Pontecorvo:* We thought about it before starting but decided against it because in checking locations we found we could rebuild without spending too much money and because making a movie creating part of the images and using another already existing part would have resulted in unevenness. It would also have taken away some creative unity.

*Interviewer: The Battle of Algiers* reveals some kind of fundamental inspiration by the cinema of Rossellini. Do you feel a sort of artistic kinship with him?

*Pontecorvo:* Yes, definitely. As a matter of fact I started working in the movies because of Rossellini. I had been tempted for a long time but I couldn't make my mind up about it. I remember I saw *Paisá* long after its release and it filled me with such enthusiasm that from that moment on I told myself "You are going to make movies." And I quit journalism for directing.

*Interviewer:* What episode of *Paisá* struck you the most?

*Pontecorvo: Po,* the sixth.

*Interviewer: The Battle of Algiers* also shows the influence of some of the great Russian directors—Eisenstein, Pudovkin. What Russian director do you feel closest to?

*Pontecorvo:* Dovzhenko.

*Interviewer:* Why?

*Pontecorvo:* For his extraordinary sweetness and humanity. However I do like the power of Eisenstein's image, although sometimes it degenerates into formalism to the detriment of the immediate communication.

*Interviewer:* Who would be your *perfect* director?

*Pontecorvo:* He would be made up of three quarters Rossellini and one quarter Eisenstein.

*Interviewer:* Seeing the last sequences of *The Battle of Algiers* reminded me of Eisenstein's famous words about *Potemkin:* "From a tiny cellular organism of the battleship to the organism of the entire battleship, from a tiny cellular organism of the fleet to the organism of the whole fleet—thus flies through the theme the revolutionary feeling of brotherhood." In those scenes you succeeded in doing the same thing; in having a kind of unceasing pulsation going from the individual to the crowd and from the crowd to the entire people.

*Pontecorvo:* As far as stylistic choice is concerned that was perhaps the only difficult scene to shoot. In the end of the movie I wanted some kind of a chant—if the word is not too exaggerated—a chant in homage to this will for living, for being free; to this choir of collective enthusiasm. I felt that this moment of the movie could only be expressed in the form of a ballet. But a ballet would pose a very difficult problem because the entire movie had been shot according to a stylistic module—as I said before—"the dictatorship of truth." So we had to keep up this stylistic consistency in this "ballet" as well. Now if you want to keep that sense of truth it is difficult to show people being physically charged by the police and at the same time moving forward and backward with the rhythm of an inner musical pulsation. I wanted a crowd which was swaying, dancing, and singing according to a precise rhythm, with a close-up of a woman, her face inspired and radiant. She would go toward the police, they would push her to the ground; she would get up and start moving forward again, they would push her back to the ground; she would get up and so on. We had shot the scene several times but it didn't ring true. Finally, we shot it to the beat of the *baba-salem,* an African percussion instrument. We thus succeeded in keeping this sense of absolute truth and at the same time attained that pulsation which is like a rapidly beating heart.

*Interviewer:* How do you shoot crowd scenes?

*Pontecorvo:* When you've got a crowd scene the easiest mistake you can make is to shoot it as such. Instead I think you should divide the work in two parts. First of all you have to know what kind of volumes you want to be seen moving, how you want them to evolve in the frame, what kind of inner relationship you want. You have to organize them or even better draw them on the ground. Next you rehearse this great movement and when you are satisfied with it you can begin shooting. The second part comes in the actual shooting where you only concentrate on the front line of the crowd, the five or six people closest to the camera. They become the focus; if someone has the wrong expression or makes an exaggerated gesture you start all over again as if they were the only ones involved. It's like being in a studio with them alone. You see you don't have to worry about what's happening behind them because while you are shooting your assistants are making sure that exactly what you had decided on in rehearsals is taking place. You can see how scenes which look as though they have been "stolen" from reality require meticulous preparation.

*Interviewer:* The factual way you shot the Algerian faces reminded me very much of Eisenstein's peasants in *Que Viva Mexico!*

*Pontecorvo:* I believe the results you call "factual" always depend exclusively on your approach. If you don't intend to emphasize local color or folklore; if you refuse to exploit exotic ugliness, but instead look for the humanity of people which is the same all over the world, in a yellow man, black, white, Italian or Arab, you can't go wrong. It's like going upstairs in the dark but having a handrail to hold on to.

*Interviewer:* How did you get that sense of surging power in the scene with the arrival of the paratroopers in Algiers?

*Pontecorvo:* It was shot from very far away with a very strong telephoto lens. It must have been the 600mm. I don't remember exactly now. Anyway, I wanted the *paras* to look like Martians— an irresistible, rhythmical, invading force whose arrival changes the balance of power. I asked Marcello Gatti to give me a completely edged-out photography, so that the faces at the beginning were unintelligible—white—until the close-up of the colonel, where they were outlined, where they came into focus. I must also say that part of the impact of the arrival is due to the fact that the scene is well placed in the screenplay; it comes at a moment when there is an absolute need for a dramatic surge ahead. We were also lucky enough to find a colonel with the right face and lucky enough to have him wear dark glasses. . . .

*Interviewer:* You were saying before that photography is almost as important for you as music. Music gives the film its dialectic, I find . . .

*Pontecorvo:* Yes, for me music is very important. I think that the cinema and musical composition have some common needs. Speaking for myself music is not only a stimulus but it provides me with an inner rhythm. I'll try to make myself clearer. I don't have great experience in cinema, having directed only four movies, so I still have some fear in shooting. In the morning when I get on the set I am not exactly carefree, and if I haven't done it before getting there, I try desperately to compose a musical theme in my mind, a piece of music which would probably be very similar to the one we'll eventually use in the movie. Since I am not a professional composer, this theme does not always come. But when it does, the fears I might have vanish and suddenly I am terribly self-confident. I know exactly what I want, the timing I need, where to set the camera, how to have the actors perform. I can even tell you more. When I am preparing a movie and a musical theme is suggested to me by a certain scene I know that it means that scene will be all right, at least for me anyway.

*Interviewer:* You also make very effective use of silence; it too seems to be very important to you. . . .

*Pontecorvo:* Silence is just like music. I'd rather talk of music and silence than music and absence of music. There is a composer I love—Webern. In his works silence has an extraordinary value. In cinema, maybe even more than in music, you come to value the importance of silence contrasted with sound; for me, alternating silence and sound counterpoints the visual image. I believe this uncompromisingly. Cinema that was born as visual image will become more and more a sound image despite those who theorize about the negative effect of music in cinema. Besides, there are moments when, by using the musical image, you can eliminate a scene, cut out some dialogue, not shoot things you had intended or shoot more than you had planned. This happened in *Burn!* For instance, I found the scene where Marlon Brando goes to free the black man, played by Evaristo Marquez, a bit wordy. Brando himself was holding back as though he were afraid of it. It's a point where there was just too much dialogue, useful dialogue, but it sort of weighs things down. Suddenly the Bach cantata "Come sweet death" occurred to me. Of course the title had nothing to do with

the scene but its theme perfectly coupled the mood I wanted. So
we took out half the dialogue and played the cantata while we
were shooting without telling Brando a thing. With such a sensitive
human being the device produced an exceptional result: Brando
was so great that at the end of the take the entire company sprang
up applauding. Naturally in the final mixing I put in the same
cantata which had saved us during the shooting. Maybe this is a
good time to make a further point about music in my work. I
think that underneath every story that the movies tell there is, when
it is there, what I call the "true story," the story which matters,
which lasts, which remains despite genre, appearance, or plot.
This "hidden" story is always the same; it is of the pain, the joy,
the fear, the strength and weakness, the fragile hopes of man—
the eternal themes of the human condition. Personally when I
succeed in expressing this "hidden" story I owe it above all else
to the intercession of music. Of course I would never dream of
theorizing about this as I am quite aware that there are some who
claim music in cinema to be neither a justified nor a correct addition. Yet sometimes, while shooting a scene, you feel as though you
are still at the surface, not making any progress—so very far from
our "hidden" story. Experience tells you that what you are making
is mechanically good, full of action and the famous, I should
really say "notorious," suspense. But in reality you know that your
imagination is not there, that the camera you've aimed on the face
of an extra, for example, is unable to find the necessary warmth to
go beyond the anonymity of that face, to find behind it what is
truly real, fragile. What you need—as in life—is to become involved with more passion, courage, and enthusiasm; to get carried
away; to linger on that face or that situation a bit longer than the
"strict" laws of rhythm and spectacle permit. At these points music
can magically intervene, giving you the necessary strength, courage, enthusiasm to break that crust of indifference through which
we generally look at others and in so doing to come in touch with
the "hidden" story, the "true" story. You see I don't take drugs,
but in a sense that's what music is for me. Having a musical theme
in mind gives me the guts to outdo myself; when I am "high"
through music I am able to do things I'd never even dream of
when "sober."

*Interviewer:* In the beginning of *The Battle of Algiers* there are also a few bars of Bach. . . .

*Pontecorvo:* Yes. A few bars of "The Passion according to Saint Matthew."

*Interviewer:* And in the torture sequences as well.

*Pontecorvo:* That's a chorale in Gregorian style which might remind you of Bach but Ennio Morricone composed it. However I do use two or three bars of Bach in all my films. I guess it's partly because of superstition but also because I am a real Bach freak. One of my children is even named Johann Sebastian—in homage.

*Interviewer:* What made you decide to have music in the torture sequences instead of realistic sounds?

*Pontecorvo:* The torture used by the French as their basic counter-guerrilla tactic is the low point of human degradation caused by the war. It seemed to me that the religious music I used in those sequences emphasized with even greater authority the gravity of that degradation. But at the same time torture creates a sort of relationship between those who do it and those who undergo it. With human pity the common bond, the music served to transcend the particular situation making them symbols of an all-encompassing characteristic—that of giving and enduring pain.

*Interviewer:* Why was the music identical for the placement of the bombs by the NLF and the *pieds noirs?*

*Pontecorvo:* Violence is seen in the entire film in an extremely painful way. Its consequences are the same even when used by those who are historically right; using it is a tragic necessity.

*Interviewer:* Do you play an instrument?

*Pontecorvo:* The piano, poorly. I began studying musical composition but had to quit after a few months. I learned practically nothing. Still what interests me most in life, what attracts me most, is music. After seeing *The Battle of Algiers* a British film critic said, "But this is a musical!" It might sound odd given the usual negative connotation of the word "musical," but that's the comment I liked best. You see those tapes on the shelf? They're the soundtracts of my documentaries and some of my films. I composed them

myself either whistling or banging away at the piano. Afterward
I had them transcribed and orchestrated.

*Interviewer:* What kind of relationship is there between a self-
taught composer like you and a Conservatory trained professional
like Ennio Morricone?

*Pontecorvo:* A great one. But this is thanks to Ennio's generosity
and personality. I don't know whether it would be the same with
other composers. For what is exceptional about Morricone, aside
from his great creative qualities, is his patience and his goodness.
Putting up with a director who wants to compose part of the music
—even a small part—really takes a saint, and I have found that
saint in Morricone. When I used to compose the music for my
documentaries I'd work with young composers just graduated from
the Conservatory who were very happy to make some money and
who'd orchestrate whatever I wanted. But when a musician who is
as important as Morricone accepts your collaboration, your bug-
ging him—because you do make him waste time—and agrees on
top of everything else to share the title credits with you—he's just
got to be as good as he is. Let me tell you what kind of fellow he
is. When we were working over the music of *The Battle of Algiers*
we had some problems in communication since it was the first time
we were working together. Those first days he came up with some
themes which just didn't quite convince me. Since Ennio is one of
the few cinema composers who knows music really well I was
rather nervous. I couldn't dare do what I had done with the others
—shamelessly whistle him a tune, saying, "Look, I'd like you to
orchestrate it." Anyway we had been working about ten days and
time was flying. The movie had already been chosen for the Venice
Film Festival and we had a deadline to meet. By that time Morricone had composed some pieces that I really liked but there was
a great deal still missing, including the protagonist's theme or the
central theme of Ali la Pointe. All of a sudden a tune which was
to become the central theme of the movie came to me. I called
Ennio and said, "I'm coming right over because I think I've got the
theme. I've tape-recorded a tune I really dig." As I got out of my
car in front of his door I just kept whistling it over and over again
without even realizing it. I kept on whistling as I rang the buzzer
and when I finally got upstairs Morricone said, "Last night I came

up with the idea for the main theme." He had a strange look on his face. "Well"—I said—"let's hear it." I wasn't terribly interested because I was so sure of my own. So he sits down at the piano and what does he play? My theme! I was flabbergasted! "Ennio," I said, "you must be joking. It's almost exactly like mine." He kept on seriously, playing the role, and replied, "Well, you know we talked about it so much . . . it was all around us . . . besides the movie itself suggested it." "Nonsense," I said, "it's the same one I thought of." And I played the tape for him. There was something I just couldn't put my finger on, just couldn't understand. I scrutinized him, wondering what was going on, but he kept a straight face. Eventually I gave up trying to solve the puzzle because somehow we had gotten the theme and that was all that really mattered. Well, the night the Golden Lion was awarded in Venice, Ennio got up at the press conference and told everyone how that night he had overheard me whistling my theme through the buzzer and had decided not to say a word to me about it unless I won the Golden Lion. Not only is he a great friend, a great man, but he has a genius for film music. His contribution in *Burn!*, for instance, was priceless. There is hardly any of my music in it, just a few bars during the killing of the black men as they come out of the cane field. And I only put it in because of superstition; until then I had always written some of the music in all my films. And speaking of *Burn!*, that's one movie that improved tremendously with the addition of his music. As a matter of fact there is even one scene that I could say *he shot himself* because the music makes such a difference. It is the meeting between Brando and Marquez; I was very unsatisfied with it. It wasn't expressing the emotions or the ideas I'd hoped it would. Well, Ennio composed the perfect piece; it gave the scene all the tension it had been missing. I now consider it one of the most beautiful and touching of the entire movie.

*Interviewer:* You never write the screenplay of your movies. Is there a difference between a film you write and a film a screenwriter writes for you? Does the extent of your creative participation in a film diminish because you don't write it?

*Pontecorvo:* Maybe in the U.S.A. directors have films written for them. In America, from what I have heard, when a producer thinks a story is good material for the film market he hires some screen-writers, has them write a script, and then chooses a director who will turn it into a movie. In Europe, however, it's a completely different thing. I don't think it is quite accurate to say that a screen-writer writes a film *for* me. As far as I am concerned the choice of a topic is the most difficult problem and that choice has never come from a producer but from me. That's one of the reasons why I only make a movie every three or four years. It takes me that long to find a story I really like. I eliminate scores of topics and ideas for topics while searching for my next project. You could say I am overly selective. At any rate, after finishing a movie I try to plan the next one by myself, then I talk about it with several screen-writers but ultimately get in touch with the one I have worked with up until now, Franco Solinas. I hold him in very high esteem not only for his capacity of judgment but for his good intuition about the choice of a topic. We then confer on the idea, and if for some reason it does not work, we'll spend weeks, months, however long is necessary, "looking around" for another. Once a theme is decided on, the next step, at least in all the films I have made so far, is documentation. I remember before beginning *The Battle of Algiers* a friend of mine put me in touch with some French officers and privates, all former parachutists, and I spent weeks taping conversations with them in Paris. Then Solinas and I went to Algiers to feel out the situation and gather further information about the NLF. We met with Algerian partisans, talked with the people of the Casbah, got direct emotions. I spent days with Sala Bazi, who had been a member of the NLF. He explained step by step how the organization functioned, how they made their bombs, placed them, etc. We came away with an idea of the situation as complete as if we had lived it ourselves. We had previously been in Algeria to get original material for *Para*. Then it was before the independence and we found ourselves in the midst of the *pieds noirs'* last stand. Between the two visits we had an enormous harvest of information. Once the documentation is finished we begin discussing the structure of the movie. What comes of that discussion is a first outline followed by a second more elaborate treatment. As you can see, *not writing* one's own movie is a far cry from not influencing the outcome of the screenplay. We keep up this discussion and exchanging of ideas even where the dialogue is concerned; when something does not suit me I ask to have it changed or change it myself while shooting. You see in Europe a director is responsible for practically every aspect of the film except the financial. Getting back to your question, I'll say no, I don't think the fact of *not writing* one's own movies changes the situation from a creative point of view. But even if the directors' work were limited to selection and refusal of material, this alone would amount to a huge creative activity.

*Interviewer:* Did you in fact make many changes during the shooting of *The Battle of Algiers?*

*Pontecorvo:* No. Up until now I have been lucky enough to work with one of the best screenwriters in Europe. And then again it's unlikely that doubts are going to spring up on the set when so much discussion takes place during the drafting. However, minor problems do arise from time to time. Instead of shooting a scene with dialogue the way you had planned, you might just focus on a face that tells you a certain something. Sometimes a location suggests a change, or a rhythm which seemed perfect on paper might no longer work, so you might decide to solve the scene in another way, with music for instance. As you know I try to shoot with a musical rhythm in mind. When dialogue collides with that rhythm and becomes superfluous, I remove it. I actually changed very little in *The Battle of Algiers.*

*Interviewer:* Scene 10 is not in the movie. Did you shoot it and edit it out or did you never shoot it at all?

*Pontecorvo:* I never shot it.

*Interviewer:* Why? By showing that life goes on in Paris as usual while Algiers is a battleground the scene emphasizes that the colonial war is almost a war by proxy which only indirectly involves the "mother country."

*Pontecorvo:* Granted. But a film enters my mind at a certain moment in its own way, with its own sounds, its own images, ratios and proportions, its own inner balance, its own wholeness. Now, even if that scene was right from a narrative point of view, I believe it would have taken something away from the compactness and the general tension of the entire movie. That's why I chose not to shoot it.

*Interviewer:* In the script an explosion takes place at a soccer stadium. Why did you change the site to a racetrack in the movie?

*Pontecorvo:* I felt that there would have been more drama, more visual beauty in showing the effect of the explosion on the horses. Furthermore, the racetrack was generally frequented by the colonialist establishment whereas it would have been like planting a bomb among the common people by having it at the soccer stadium.

*Interviewer:* Were there any other professional actors aside from Jean Martin who plays Colonel Mathieu?

*Pontecorvo:* No.

*Interviewer:* Where did you find him?

*Pontecorvo:* In Paris. He was a little-known theater actor and I chose him because he had the perfect build. We tested a number of people, even one of our extras, but none was physically imposing enough.

*Interviewer:* Did any of the actors you took from the street ask to read the screenplay before deciding to work with you?

*Pontecorvo:* Yes, some of the Europeans. They were mostly French who had come to Algeria after independence.

*Interviewer:* Why did you decide to have Yacef Saadi play himself in the movie?

*Pontecorvo:* Simply because his face happened to be perfect for the part, not because it had been his real-life role. In fact, I am usually very negative about that type of casting.

*Interviewer:* What problems did you have directing someone in the role he had lived?

*Pontecorvo:* It was slightly more complicated directing Saadi because he was a bit ill at ease playing himself and had to overcome a certain amount of embarrassment. That's all.

*Interviewer:* Did you use anyone else in the movie who had actually taken part in the battle of Algiers?

*Pontecorvo:* Yes, I did. And sometimes this caused problems because they'd want us to emphasize aspects of the re-enactment which seemed important to them but which didn't have anything to do with the overall structural development.

*Interviewer:* Was there major trouble directing people who had never even seen a camera before?

*Pontecorvo:* In a film like *The Battle of Algiers* acting is not so important as you might think; this type of story demands much less individual technique. The face is what really counts.

*Interviewer:* Did you politically motivate the actors in any way?

*Pontecorvo:* With some it was useful to do so while with others it was not necessary because they were even more politicized than we. Then, there were those who didn't give a damn about what we were trying to say, so any motivation of that sort would have been pointless.

*Interviewer:* How do you explain a scene to an actor?

*Pontecorvo:* I show it to him myself. Yet, I get so terribly embarrassed when I am obliged to act out a scene that I have my assistants make the rest of the company turn around and look the other way.

*Interviewer:* Where did you find the fellow who plays Ali la Pointe?

*Pontecorvo:* He was an illiterate peasant we found in a marketplace. We chose him because of his resemblance to the real Ali and more importantly because he looked like *my* idea of Ali.

*Interviewer:* How did you get him to act?

*Pontecorvo:* It wasn't easy—he was terrified by the camera. We had to repeat things time and again showing him the direction for his glances, giving him all sorts of points of reference. I'd say that in the beginning he didn't really act; but instead let us use the expression in those extraordinary eyes as well as the instinctive dramatic quality and natural tension of his face.

*Interviewer:* And when he had to act in more difficult scenes, when he talks for instance. . . .

*Pontecorvo:* Well, at times, we had to construct his acting in a mechanical way. I'll give you an example. You know if you look at the ground for a tenth of a second and then quickly raise your glance to eye level it gives the face an expression of doubt or it seems as though a thought has crossed your mind. This is what I had Ali do, showing him with a mark on the ground just where he was supposed to look, until he'd repeat it mechanically—thus I'd construct his acting bit by bit. I know it's a horrible method but you have to use it when you can't obtain results any other way. I should add, though, that after the first weeks of shooting it was possible to communicate emotions to him through analogy and have him reproduce them. Then the results were obviously much better.

*Interviewer:* Would you have preferred a big name in *The Battle of Algiers* like Brando in *Burn!?*

*Pontecorvo:* No, I wouldn't have. For reasons of verisimilitude it was better to use unknowns in *The Battle of Algiers.* And I think it'll be the same for my movie on Christ.

*Interviewer:* Do you prefer working with non-actors?

*Pontecorvo:* No, I'd rather work with professionals as they give you more; a non-actor can't give you those exceptional moments of a Brando, even if he gives other things. I'd say that the two are as different as a Stradivarius and a dime-store violin. However in cinema—unlike theater where you obviously have completely different problems—the somatic component, the face, is at times more important than the ability to act. And it's easier to find someone who looks like the character you have in mind from among millions of people than from the relatively small group who are professional actors. So if I don't find the face which suits me among the actors, I start combing the streets.

*Interviewer:* Obviously you think that anybody can act. . . .

*Pontecorvo:* Yes, of course. All it takes is a director who has enough film and enough patience. And I am always ready with both. Besides it is easier to work with a non-actor than with a professional because he does not balk at repeating a scene twenty-five times if necessary.

*Interviewer:* What is the best way for you to use an actor?

*Pontecorvo:* When you're working you have an image or a model of the character you want the actor to represent. I think you have to make the most of the actor's inventive capability and gestural spontaneity within the framework of your model. I am hated by some actors, by one in particular, because he says I allow him too little artistic freedom. I don't agree. I believe I leave a fair amount of invention up to the actor while keeping in mind that acting is only one of the components of a movie—not *the* only one. At times individual creativity must be sacrificed to other needs—the story, the dialogue, the music, and so on.

*Interviewer:* I think Brando is the actor you're hinting at. He said he "could kill you!" because you hampered his creativity and made him repeat the same scene dozens of times under the scorching sun.

*Pontecorvo:* I know he accused me of that but I don't think it's true. Brando is a brilliant and sensitive actor and I can understand why he didn't feel at ease with me—he wasn't accustomed to the way European directors work. He's also a supersensitive man and anything bothers him; any kind of external pressure is a burden for him. But a director has to exert at least a minimum amount of outside pressure, otherwise every actor would do what he wants— it would be like sailing without a helm, you'd go where the wind takes you. Anyway, to defend myself, let me say that if I were interested in manipulating actors I would certainly never have chosen such an exceptional one as Brando to do it with.

*Interviewer:* What part did editing play in *The Battle of Algiers?*

*Pontecorvo:* A very small one, although it turned out to be a difficult task. The editor we started out with wanted to do a classical cutting job, while I wanted it to look as though it had been "stolen" from reality. We couldn't agree, so we ended our collaboration. Next, we de-edited and re-edited with Mario Morra, who today is one of the best in Italy. At that time he was a young editor just starting out and *The Battle of Algiers* was his first important project. Needless to say, he dedicated himself to the job with tremendous enthusiasm. Thanks to him we were able to edit the movie in a way which corresponded with the screenplay, the shooting, etc.; it looked as though it had literally been "stolen" from reality. To achieve this effect you have to digress from the usual cutting order, long shot, medium-long shot, etc. You must, in fact, establish a new order.

*Interviewer:* Was there any pressure during the editing to smooth out angles or delete anything, considering the hell raised by the French?

*Pontecorvo:* No. I was absolutely free—you must have freedom all the time, even then. *Nobody* should have access to the editing room.

*Interviewer:* How about the producers?

*Pontecorvo:* Least of all the producers! They're a public menace! Naturally you can demand this in Europe but it is different in the States where the role of the producer changes. Anyway I don't think they should ever have a say—even in the final outcome. I can only restate what I believe—a movie must mirror the virtues and defects of only one person, its director. Although it is a collaborative effort by many—the screenwriter, composer, director of photography—he alone is ultimately responsible. No. Nobody can tell you how to edit your movie, least of all the producer. The director must be free to choose what he likes, making all the blunders that anyone performing a creative activity can make. Then and only then will the film have an identity and not be another "product." Of course if you are interested in manufacturing "products," then the producer could be helpful to you. Personally I don't subscribe to the theory even though I do recognize it as a defensible one. At any rate in a film where the director is making a personal statement it would be disastrous to let the producer stick his nose in the cutting room.

*Interviewer: The Battle of Algiers* was dubbed in Italy, while in the U.S.A., for instance, it was not. Obviously its impact is much greater in the original version. If possible, would you have left the movie in its original French and Arabic?

*Pontecorvo:* No, you know that not dubbing in Italy would have meant having only one tenth of its audience. Besides, even in the dubbed version there were lots of things left in Arabic.

*Interviewer:* Some detractors say you procrastinate about making new movies because of all your prizes and previous successes.

*Pontecorvo:* In the first place I don't think prizes or awards are important. There are other, more meaningful criteria for judging a film's worth. And the time lapse between films is not due to any fear of comparison with my "so-called" successes, as some of my colleagues would charge. Just look at my first two films as an example. *The Long Blue Road* wasn't very successful at all and yet four years went by before *Kapo.* During that time I had many offers to make movies but turning them out one after the other is not the point. You can't compare shooting a story you really love and feel is yours to one you're only remotely interested in—the one gives you emotion and pleasure, the other nothing. I think it's better to make less money and live more modestly, shooting only when you are convinced of what you are doing right or wrong.

*Interviewer:* Jack Nicholson, actor-director and part of the new American cinema, is reported to have said in *Ramparts* that it is possible to make movies like *The Battle of Algiers* in Italy because of the support of the Communist Unions. Would you like to comment on this?

*Pontecorvo:* Neither Communist Unions nor the Communist Party had anything to do with *The Battle of Algiers,* nor, as far as I know, with any other Italian political film. But I don't think this has any bearing on a film anyway. You've got to convince a producer that your movie will make a profit—that's what's important. When I took the screenplay around, the major distributors said they would have backed any other film of mine but that—and not for political reasons, but because "Nobody is interested in Arabs." They also thought "It's not fictionalized enough . . . you don't want to use professional actors. . . ." Can you imagine Rizzoli offered me a minimum guarantee of sixty-five thousand dollars— that's absolutely ridiculous!

*Interviewer:* How much did *The Battle of Algiers* cost?

*Pontecorvo:* Between seven and eight hundred thousand dollars. Aside from the money, Rizzoli told me, "Look, I've got a stack of scripts here. Pick any one and we'll make it—I *want* to make a

movie with you, just not *that* one. Do you think I'm crazy?" You
see there were obstacles of this kind. Producers weren't eager to
make political films because they didn't think they'd make money.
*The Battle of Algiers* was probably the first Italian or even European political film. Now, of course, things are different. Producers
understand that these films do make money, that there is a market
for them, so they are the first to suggest them. The American audience, unlike the French or Italian, probably is not yet ready for
political topics. However, I am convinced that there'll soon be
enough public interest in these themes for political movies to be
made there too. Then, of course, producers will be quite happy to
back them. Just one word about the Unions by the way. Our relationship with them was rather strained during the making of *The
Battle of Algiers* because due to budget limitations the company
had to be much smaller than the regulation number.

*Interviewer:* What are your views on the connection between politics and cinema?

*Pontecorvo:* It is such a broad topic we could go on discussing it
until next week and I don't think you'd feel like doing that. In
one sentence, I can say that you mustn't overrate the importance of
cinema on politics. Cinema is one of various means which contribute to the advancement of certain ideas. Lenin used to say that
from among all the arts film is the most important for the oppressed classes—but from among *all the arts*. The experiences that
really matter are those the masses live directly. This seems self-
evident yet not all "committed directors" appear to be convinced
about it. I believe film's limitation lies in its not being able to
penetrate deeply. Instead, it "communicates," raising nothing
more than emotions.

*Interviewer:* There is a polemic against the political film which
runs: "You can't make a politically serious movie with capital-
ist money"—a film is judged by the source of its production
money. . . .

*Pontecorvo:* The polemic is the result of "political infantilism."
They should remember what Lenin said about the inner contradictions of capitalism that take place at every level, even the very
low one we are now considering. I think a producer would back

a movie that slanders both his mother and father if he knew it would make a profit. You see, I am deeply convinced that the establishment fully understands the limitations of political films. As we said before, a film is not the revolution. If the day comes that political films are mass produced, thus becoming a potential threat, the establishment will try to put an end to them. This possibility, though, is much more remote than any neo-revolutionists might theorize about from their rostrums.

*Interviewer:* Do you think the political film can perform the didactic task of spreading certain ideas which neither the political novel nor political theater has succeeded in doing?

*Pontecorvo:* The main difference between political novels and political films is the film's larger circulation. Otherwise the differences all weigh against cinema because its communication is only skin deep. Novels stimulate people to think more, and reading is essentially a more profound experience.

*Interviewer:* Why then make political movies?

*Pontecorvo:* Cinema can be a way of revitalizing a people's deadened responses. We have been conditioned to absorb a false vision of reality that is dominated by the tastes, morals, and perceptions of the "establishment." To forego the possibility of opposing the *fictions* diffused by this establishment is in the least irresponsible. That is why I believe in a cinema which addresses itself to the masses and not a cinema *d'élite* for an elite.

# Franco Solinas

One of the most highly regarded screenwriters in the world, Franco Solinas lives all year round in Fregene, a small seaside resort half an hour's drive from Rome. He is of medium height, with a trim muscular body, and has the look of an outdoors man, the scorched face of those who live by the sea. His manner is composed, somewhat reserved, with an occasional smile flashing across an intense countenance. He strikes you as keen and perceptive with a gift for understated humor.

After a seafood lunch at a nearby *trattoria* we return to his beautiful, white, A-frame house built right by the water. There we have coffee in a living room whose huge windows command an endless view of the sea, gray on this rainy April afternoon. It is cozy, quiet, inviting conversation.

Talking about his own work Franco Solinas is lucid and self-critical. He speaks in a smooth, clear voice. His sentences are sharp, precise, well-balanced. History and politics fascinate him deeply. The expression "political films" has come to be synonymous with his name—for years they have been the only films he has been willing to write. One French critic has observed, "In his work with directors Rosi and Pontecorvo, Franco Solinas has perhaps discovered a new way of writing history."

Born in Sardinia in January 1927, he left the island during World War II and went to Rome where at sixteen he joined the Resistance. At the end of the war he became a member of the Italian Communist Party. He then worked his way through the University, receiving a law degree he has never used. While a student he held a number of jobs, construction worker, office clerk, tutor, traveling salesman; at that time he also started writing short stories which appeared in Italian newspapers and magazines, and in the early fifties he began working as a screenwriter.

His successful collaboration with Pontecorvo began with his original screenplay for *Giovanna*. It continued with *The Long Blue Road*, an adaptation of his own novel *Squarció* (The Rift), a study in the life of a poacher. It was published in 1957 and contained the seeds of his favorite theme, "man observed against the

*Note.* The editor and screenwriter are not related.

background of a collective situation." He then went on to Ponte-corvo's *Kapo, The Battle of Algiers,* and *Burn!* He also co-authored screenplays for Roberto Rossellini's *Vanina Vanini* and Francesco Rosi's *Salvatore Giuliano.* With *Quien Sabe?* he fathered the "po-litical western." He has written screenplays for other major directors, including the recent *Life Is Like a Train, Like a Train* to be done by Sam Peckinpah.

In the middle of April 1972 when this interview took place, Franco Solinas was about to leave for Chile where French director Costa Gavras was to begin shooting his script *State of Siege.* P.N.S.

# The Interview

*Interviewer:* Over lunch you said that around the time of *Para* and afterward with *The Battle of Algiers* you felt that colonialism was a most urgent theme. What in particular made you feel that way?

*Solinas:* The times we were living in. They were times when Euro-pean politics were stagnating for two main reasons. First, the work-ing class was thought of as completely integrated, it seemed non-existent in relation to the revolutionary cause. Second, a deep anal-ysis of the political situation had completely ruled out the possibility of a revolution on our continent. You can understand how the ex-plosions of colonial contradictions, the revolutions, the armed struggles that then were erupting from Cuba to Algeria in the entire geography of the Third World stirred up hope as well as interest. You had come to believe that capitalism seemingly un-defeatable at home could have been defeated once and for all in its supplying bases. In a way it was the same hope that was later to be theorized on the one hand by Lin Piao with the strategy of "the country and the city" and on the other by Frantz Fanon's proposal to abandon the traditional models and means in the con-struction of a different civilization.

*Interviewer:* How then did you view colonialism?

*Solinas:* As a confrontation between the human reality of a country of the Third World awakening to history through sufferings, hardship, ugliness, racial and physical destruction and Europe, a race that had been able to become handsome, elegant, refined at the other's expense. I was not simply trying to show that colonialism is wrong, since that is a fact that colonialists themselves agree upon. Instead I was interested in the relationship of two conflicting forces and the technique used to resolve their confrontation.

*Interviewer:* Can we assume you had a didactic intention preparing the movie?

*Solinas:* Yes, sure. I was intrigued by the mechanism of the struggle against colonialism and in particular by its manifestation in Algiers through tactics of urban guerrilla warfare. I meant to explain these tactics, the details of their function, by taking them apart from within to show how the mechanisms work. You could say that our goal was not guerrilla for the sake of the spectacle but the use of spectacle to teach the guerrilla.

*Interviewer:* Why choose France to represent one of the two sides of that confrontation?

*Solinas:* Well, after analyzing several colonial situations France appeared to embody the terms of one half of our dialectic. She was at the same time a colonial power and the most representative example of the bourgeoisie, the Enlightenment, the French Revolution. Politically she posed a contradiction between the slogans, phrases, rhetoric—in other words the form of the bourgeois revolution—and its contents—the everyday practice of domination, oppression, torture.

*Interviewer:* How much of the *Para* script was used in *The Battle of Algiers?*

*Solinas:* None. It only provided the fundamental inspiration, the conflict between Western civilization and the filth of the colonial regime.

*Interviewer:* Did the Algerians exert any pressure as far as the political weight of the story goes?

*Solinas:* None whatever. Let's just say that they might have preferred a more traditionally heroic film.

*Interviewer:* What were your most important sources of documentation?

*Solinas:* The newspapers and the police records of the day, the books written in France and Algeria, and the theories of French colonels.

*Interviewer:* What theories?

*Solinas:* In Indochina the French had discovered Mao's writing on guerrilla warfare and General Giap's techniques and strategies. Of course they tried to theorize a counterguerrilla strategy in Algeria. They even obtained some results, but their strategy had a major shortcoming—their counterguerrilla warfare had no ties with the people. It was a purely abstract theory divorced from any national reality. That's why, even using Mao's and Giap's techniques in reverse, they couldn't have won in the long run. And in effect, they didn't, even though they did win the battle of Algiers.

*Interviewer:* Who is Colonel Mathieu?

*Solinas:* Mathieu sums up the personalities of three or four colonels who actually existed. He is a kind of improved synthesis in that each individual colonel was much less lucid and alert. Mathieu is not a realistic character in the traditional sense but rather embodies a realistic idea: "the rationality" that supports a certain kind of society and should not be ignored. In order to expose the principles of that "rationality" in the film the character of Mathieu must demystify the intermediate, rhetorical, contradictory, sentimental positions that usually mask the reality. Mathieu's straightforwardness exposes the unstated "rational" aspects of civilization that France, for one, never officially recognized.

*Interviewer:* Mathieu seems too respectable, too much of a gentleman in fatigues, excessively noble. He is elegant, cultured. . . .

*Solinas:* There was no intention to create nobility. Mathieu is elegant and cultured because Western civilization is neither inelegant nor stupid.

*Interviewer:* Perhaps he is a bit too logical. . . .

*Solinas:* Why? The enemy, too, possesses logic which must not be ignored or underestimated.

*Interviewer:* Yes, but his is a form of logic which concludes that even torture is necessary and acceptable.

*Solinas:* Of course, but you don't attack colonialism for using torture. If you like, you can call torture only the "signal" indicating a decaying situation; but do not wait for the exposure of torture to become aware of the colonial situation. If you do, you are both irresponsible and naïve. The Algerian colonial situation was rotten long before torture became an issue. The truth of the matter is that France never considered the problem. The colonial situation interested her only indirectly and vaguely. Even the French Left held an ambiguous position regarding the problem. Suddenly the question of torture explodes and in France they say it's *unethical* to torture. Then and only then is the Algerian war a "dirty war," colonialism wrong, and the French position anti-historical. In my opinion this kind of reasoning is hypocritical because war is *not* ethics, war is *not* fair play. You can find the same attitude in the U.S. now where every once in a while people remember to be shocked by Vietnam. They are shocked by the occasional newspaper disclosures about the shattering effect of some of the weapons being used in the war. Yet they never really question the war itself. Once it was napalm or the defoliants, then the plastic pellet bombs or carpet bombing. Those plastic pellets, for example, are not detected by X-rays and inevitably cause death. It is the same attitude—a romantic, nineteenth-century attitude—that led to the Geneva Convention which established the rules for the kinds of bullets allowed in war. For instance the dum-dum bullet is not permitted. Bullets must have a copper nose which, unlike lead, has some solidity and does not expand upon hitting the bones. Thus, only if a man is wounded in a vital part does he die; if he's wounded in non-vital parts he survives. This kind of reasoning is ridiculous. For centuries they've tried to prove that war is fair play, just like duels; but war is not and therefore any method

used to fight it is good. When French Intelligence proved that the
Algerians also used torture—and they did too—the entire group
of French intellectuals was again shocked and began saying,
"Well, if the Algerians do it too, then. . . ." So the discussion
was again about fair play. But that's not the point. It is not a question of ethics or fair play. What we must attack is war itself and
the situations that lead to it, not the methods used to fight it.
Actually, Mathieu is extremely sincere when he rationally and
pitilessly says that torture is inevitable and that those who want a
French Algeria must steel themselves to it. If his position is im-
moral and inhuman because it tries to halt a historical process,
at least he is honest in his dishonesty. He dispenses with hypocrisy.
He has no use for it.

*Interviewer:* In the movie the French only use torture against supposed NLF members, and then according to an understandable
military strategy. Mathieu puts it this way: "Our method is interrogation and interrogation becomes a method when conducted in a
manner so as to obtain a result—that is, an answer." Yet we know
that the *paras* deliberately and indiscriminately did horrible things
in Algeria against men, women, children. . . .

*Solinas:* Don't you see that you are still making a distinction between kinds of torture. Torture is torture whether the victim be man,
woman, or child. The question of deliberately and indiscriminately
using torture or any other war method, for that matter, is that if
you do not you might *lose* the war. Naturally the French General
Staff would have never honestly tolerated the rapes that took place
in Algeria, the *paras* cutting open the bellies of pregnant women
and so on. And if they had found out about these things they would
probably have said, "What can you expect, that's war." And they
would have been right. The story had to be told from a rational
point of view based upon the logic of the events rather than upon
their appearance. And as I was saying before, I felt compelled
to present the events in this light because my position was against
a hypocritical, phony, romantic, fictionalized idea of war.

*Interviewer:* Why make Colonel Mathieu an enemy who is not
hateful?

*Solinas:* I don't believe in depicting the enemy as hateful. I think that hating enemies becomes inevitable because a beastly mechanism is set in motion in the day-to-day struggle for survival which you find in a warlike environment. You can say that the Algerian partisan hated the French youth *du contingent* the same way the Vietcong hates the G.I.—but then I wonder, does he really? Let's assume he does—and kills him. If you remove him from a situation which he himself did not choose, that hate becomes wrong and senseless. On the historical level there is no hate; problems are confronted in a different manner.

*Interviewer:* Obviously Colonel Mathieu represents France and Ali la Pointe Algeria. But why choose a pure fighter, a man with no ideology at all for the latter?

*Solinas:* Because in the Algerian revolution in place of an ideology we find a colonial reality that could no longer express itself, that could not last, that had become unbearable for the Algerians. The NLF began without any political theory. Unlike the situation in Vietnam today, for example, in Algeria at the time of the battle of Algiers the Communist Party no longer existed. It had long since been absorbed or eliminated. The only branch of the NLF which had a political program was the federation of the Algerians in France. Metropolitan France had afforded them the opportunity to develop more sophisticated political ideas, ideas with socialist leanings.

*Interviewer:* There were other revolutionary movements in Algeria, the M.N.A. for instance; they are never mentioned in the movie so that the role of the NLF seems monolithic. . . .

*Solinas:* The reason is that those groups were eliminated long before the battle of Algiers. Their leaders were either terrorized or killed by the NLF. The battle of Algiers was fought by the NLF alone, and as a matter of fact with disagreement among its leaders. The so-called "historical leaders" of the Algerian revolution, except for Ben M'Hidi, considered the battle of Algiers a political error. They were against assaults and terrorism.

*Interviewer:* In the movie the Algerians' indiscriminate assaults follow the placement of a bomb in rue de Thèbes by the Assistant

Commissioner. In a sense you could say they were justified. Was this the real sequence of events?

*Solinas:* Yes. Until the Assistant Commissioner's act of terrorism which cost thirty-two lives the NLF assaults were directed at the police or against traitors, and never at the European population indiscriminately. The bombings at the Milk Bar, Air France, etc. all followed that first one in rue de Thèbes.

*Interviewer:* Many factors that helped Algeria carry its revolution ahead are never mentioned. To quote a few: the fact that the war was costing France six hundred million dollars a month (and the battle of Algiers was causing that figure to rise daily) bleeding its economy dry, that Tunisia was helping Algeria. . . . It is somewhat biased to show the Algerians fighting solely with their own means.

*Solinas:* Yes, this is perhaps biased; yet the most important fact among all others which the film intends to emphasize is the reason for Algeria's final victory—armed struggle. I am convinced that Algeria did win with its own means because if the Algerians had not acted as they acted, suffered as they suffered, resisted and fought as they did, then Algeria might still be French today. But it is also true that the events did not take place in a crystal ball unaffected by other factors on the international scene.

*Interviewer:* In the movie the UN is presented as completely useless. It is also biased to attack the UN since the UN played more than one role in the Algerian revolution and in one of these was actually in favor of the Algerians.

*Solinas:* Yes, this is true. But here too the emphasis was on stressing the vital importance of armed struggle. The UN's usefulness—when indeed the UN can be useful—takes too long for the people to wait.

*Interviewer:* Did you intend it to be a Marxist movie?

*Solinas:* I used Marxist procedures in preparing and writing the film. So for me *The Battle of Algiers* is the result of those procedures: an analysis of two conflicting forces motivated by contingent rather than idealistic terms.

*Interviewer:* An Italian movie critic who belongs to an extreme left group has written that General De Gaulle liked *The Battle of Algiers,* implying that it was even accepted by rightists.

*Solinas:* I don't know whether or not De Gaulle liked the movie but I wouldn't be shocked if he did. I do know for a fact that the French government would not allow its release in France for five years. Besides, my point is that there are infinite ways to represent reality. Once you choose to represent it in a certain way, it can never be repudiated—not even by someone with opposite views. Anyway De Gaulle was not the average representative of the opposition because you can't forget that he had the intelligence to put an end to the Algerian situation. In any case an acceptable piece of criticism would use other criteria; however, if you want to continue along those lines, I should say that many revolutionary movements throughout the world have taken the film and made good use of it. This is far more important to me than any opinion De Gaulle might have had about *The Battle of Algiers.*

*Interviewer:* Why do you write political films? Is it because of your militancy in the Communist Party?

*Solinas:* I don't believe that a sense of mission exists for me or that I am motivated to write political films because of my political militancy. The topic that interests me most is politics. If we talked about obligation or duty it would mean that a Communist intellectual had given up his freedom, while on the contrary the work of a Communist intellectual can only be the result of his own free ideal choice.

*Interviewer:* Do you think that political films can be of political usefulness?

*Solinas:* Let's first say that movies have an accessory and not a decisive usefulness in the various events and elements that contribute to the transformation of society. It is naïve to believe that you can start a revolution with a movie and even more naïve to theorize about doing so. Political films are useful on the one hand if they contain a correct analysis of reality and on the other if they are made in such a way to have that analysis reach the largest possible audience.

*Interviewer:* How do you go about writing a movie?

*Solinas:* I never begin with a mechanical idea or situation but with a theme, usually a political topic—although I have written some more commercial products for survival or just for fun. After finding a theme and, as in *The Battle of Algiers,* a long period of information gathering, I write an outline. Then I expand the story and write the screenplay in a narrative form, as if it were a novel. I write in a way that compensates for my frustrations at being an ex-novelist and offers a number of suggestions, tips, to the director. In my screenplays I write exactly what has to be seen. I use certain descriptions, express certain states of mind, maybe give the sense of landscape, or add a detail that might make you smile since it does not exactly belong in a screenplay. But I do so because I like to think that these tips are enriching when compared to a sketchy presentation.

*Interviewer:* When we were talking earlier you mentioned that you write your films on a blackboard. How do you do it? There is not too much room on a blackboard. . . .

*Solinas:* When I work at the blackboard I jot down flashes of ideas—police, city, police patrolling city—so that I am able to see the succession of facts, the probability and timing of the story, the audience's interest, and so on. I don't write about "characters" but about facts, so by using a blackboard I can exercise visual control. This is possible also because the films I write have an extremely rational structure; they are a lot more precise than they seem in their final form where they are somewhat "polished." After writing this first synthesis I start all over again, expanding the central theme. It is still in a concise way, unfinished with points left to solve and clarify. Then I leave the blackboard and write the script and new problems arise. Working in detail what constituted a scene on the blackboard, in the script might be handled as a few lines of dialogue. The opposite is also true: what had been a few lines of dialogue could be worked into a whole scene.

*Interviewer:* Did you ever consider directing a movie—*The Battle of Algiers,* for example?

*Solinas:* Years ago when I realized that the novel was no longer important, that fiction, generally speaking, was no longer enough—

and this position hinges on my political beliefs—and I turned to the movies, I never considered directing. I chose to be a screenwriter because I am a writer and I enjoy writing. Besides you must also remember that when I began working in cinema directors and screenwriters existed as separate entities—it was almost a fixed rule that you couldn't do both. A couple of years ago I became aware of just how much screenwriting is a halfway thing, how limited a say one has in the realization of the script, how the creative process is carried only to a certain point and no further. Then there are the inevitable conflicts with the director, the difficulty in finding a director who can adapt his way of thinking to yours and vice versa. So you begin to think maybe. . . . But as time goes by it becomes increasingly difficult to make a choice like that—to direct. You need know-how, ways to get things moving. . . . Besides, I must admit that I never think about directing a movie until after I have written it. If they told me to direct *The Battle of Algiers* when I started writing it, I would have refused, because at that point I am only interested in writing. However, once the screenplay is written, I sometimes do get the urge to direct it myself. I'd have to approach it very cautiously, humbly, because frankly I am not sure how good a director I'd be. In any event I inevitably think about it when the script is finished; maybe it is because I feel closer to the film then.

*Interviewer:* You just finished writing a movie. Is it political?

*Solinas:* Yes, it is. It is a story based on an actual chronicle which took place in Latin America a few years ago, a story that tries to explain some of the ways used by imperialism to penetrate, dominate, and, when it succeeds, alter the reality of Latin America today.

# Afterword

Violent reaction to *The Battle of Algiers* came even before its completion. Quarrels started over the rumors that excerpts from the movie might be presented in 1966 on *Zoom*, a popular French TV program. The Association of the Repatriated from Algeria, the *pieds noirs*, stepped in with immediate action. While the Association's parliamentary representative reminded the government of its voting strength in the upcoming elections, its general secretary issued a public memo which demanded the prohibition "of showing, in our country, even excerpts from a movie that reflects revolting cynicism and risks inciting feelings of hatred that could be *regrettable*." The French government readily acquiesced, assuring the *pieds noirs* that a TV showing "had never even been dreamed of" and forbidding the film's theater release in France. Polemics raged when, despite diplomatic pressures, Gillo Pontecorvo's movie was invited to the 1966 Venice Film Festival and won its highest award, The Golden Lion. The French delegation defiantly filed out of both the screening and the award ceremony. The French press crackled with irritation and dismissed the film with chauvinistic arguments. Reacting to what it viewed as blatant partisanship, *Le Figaro* wrote: "the film deserved at most a chocolate medal." *L'Aurore* complained that "the most important prize went to a movie whose merits are quite questionable and which deals with a very painful moment of French history." *Combat* headlined an angry first-page article, "Venice: a rascals' verdict." *Le Monde* wrote that "the jurors' political opinions have determined the awarding of the prizes." When the French press regained some of its critical detachment its articles were once more professional, in many cases appreciative and even openly laudatory. But lately the polemics have been strongly rekindled by the publication in 1971 of General Jacques Massu's defense of the French record in Algeria, *La vraie bataille d'Alger*. P.N.S.

# Selected Bibliography

| | | |
|---|---|---|
| Argentieri, M. | RINASCITA | (Rome) Sept. 3, 1966 |
| Baker, P. | FILMS AND FILMING | (London) Nov. 1966, p. 49 |
| Bayardi, A. | NOVIDADES | (Mexico, D. F.) Dec. 11, 1966 |
| Benayun, R. | POSITIF | (Paris) 1966, no. 80, pp. 20–23 |
| Benedetti, A. | L'ESPRESSO | (Rome) Oct. 6, 1966 |
| Bianchi, P. | IL GIORNO | (Milan) Sept. 1, 1966 |
| Billard, P. | L'EXPRESS | (Paris) Sept. 11, 1966 |
| Biner, P. | JOURNAL DE GENÈVE | (Geneva) Sept. 11, 1966 |
| Bini, L. | LETTURE | (Milan) 1966, no. 10 pp. 707–710 |
| Biraghi, G. | IL MESSAGGERO | (Rome) Sept. 10, 1966 |
| Brunetta, G. P. | CINEMA E FILM | (Rome) 1966/67, no. 1, pp. 115–117 |
| Bruno, E. | FILMCRITICA | (Rome) 1966, no. 172, pp. 511–512 |
| Bruno, E. (ed.) | FILM DISCUSSI INSIEME CENTRO CULTURALE SAN FEDELE | (Milan) 1967, pp. 37–58 |
| Buache, F. | LA TRIBUNE DE LAUSANNE | (Lausanne) April 16, 1967 |
| Caldiron, O. | CIVILTÀ DELL'IMMAGINE | (Bologna) 1967, no. 3, pp. 24–27 |
| Carrol, K. | DAILY NEWS | (New York) Sept. 21, 1967 |
| Casiraghi, U. | L'UNITÀ | (Milan) Sept. 1, 1967 |
| Castellani, L. | LA RIVISTA DEL CINEMATOGRAFO | (Rome) 1966, nos. 9–10, pp. 592–596 |

| Cederna, C. | L'ESPRESSO | (Rome) Sept. 11, 1966 |
|---|---|---|
| Chapier, H. | COMBAT | (Paris) Sept. 12, 1966 |
| Chauvet, L. | LE FIGARO | (Paris) Sept. 12, 1966 |
| Ciment, L. | IMAGE ET SON | (Paris) 1966, p. 181 |
| Clemente, M. | LA FIERA LET-TERARIA | (Rome) Sept. 22, 1966 |
| Clurman, H. | THE NATION | (New York) Oct. 9, 1967 |
| Cournot, M. | LE NOUVEL OBSERVA-TEUR | (Paris) 1966, no. 96 |
| Crowther, B. | THE NEW YORK TIMES | Sept. 21, 1967 |
| Crowther, B. | THE NEW YORK SUNDAY TIMES | Oct. 1, 1967 |
| Daniel, G. | LE NOUVEL OBSERVATEUR | (Paris) 1967, p. 130 |
| Delmas, J. | JEUNE CINÉMA | (Paris) 1966, no. 17, pp. 4–6 |
| Del Re, G. | IL MESSAGGERO | (Rome) Sept. 11, 1966 |
| Disnan, F. | IL GIORNALE D'ITALIA | (Rome) Sept. 11, 1966 |
| Fofi, G. | I QUADERNI PIACENTINI | (Piacenza) 1967, no. 29, pp. 97–98 |
| Gallico, L. | L'UNITÀ | (Milan) June 21, 1966 |
| Galluzzo, T. | THE MOTION PICTURE HERALD | (New York) Sept. 21, 1967 |
| Gelmis, J. | NEWSDAY | (New York) Sept. 21, 1967 |
| Gelmis, J. | NEWSDAY | (New York) Sept. 26, 1967 |
| Gervais, G. | JEUNE CINÉMA | (Paris) 1966, no. 17, pp. 7–9 |
| Gobetti, P. | RESISTENZA, GIU-STIZIA E LIBERTÀ | (Turin) 1966, no. 10 |

| | | |
|---|---|---|
| Grazzini, G. | IL CORRIERE DELLA SERA | (Milan) Sept. 1, 1966 |
| Killingsworth, K. | THE DAILY AMERICAN | (Rome) Nov. 11, 1966 |
| Korn, K. | FRANKFURTER ALL-GEMEINE ZEITUNG | (Frankfurt) Sept. 2, 1967/68, pp. 27–31 |
| Kozloff, M. | FILM QUARTERLY | (U.C.L.A.) Winter 1966 |
| Laura, E. G. | L'OSSERVATORE RO-MANO | (Rome) Sept. 2, 1966 |
| Liverani, M. | MOMENTO SERA | (Rome) Sept. 1, 1966 |
| Lori, S. | ROMA | (Naples) Sept. 1, 1966 |
| Martin, M. | CINÉMA 66 | (Paris) 1966, no. 110, pp. 87–90 |
| Mazars, P. | LE FIGARO LIT-TÉRAIRE | (Paris) Sept. 8, 1966 |
| Miccicchè, L. | L'AVANTI | (Milan) Sept. 1, 1966 |
| Milne, T. | SIGHT AND SOUND | (London) Autumn 1966, p. 175 |
| Moravia, A. | L'ESPRESSO | (Rome) Oct. 10, 1966 |
| Morgenstern, J. | NEWSWEEK | (New York) Oct. 23, 1967 |
| Narbone, J. | CAHIERS DU CINÉMA | (Paris) 1966, no. 183, pp. 25–26 |
| Neuvecelle, J. | FRANCE SOIR | (Paris) Sept. 1, 1966 |
| Nuñez y Lobator | EXCELSIOR | (Mexico) Dec. 9, 1966 |
| Pado, D. | L'AURORE | (Paris) Sept. 12, 1966 |
| Pillitteri, P. | L'AVANTI | (Milan) Sept. 1, 1966 |
| Pontecorvo, G. | LES LETTRES FRAN-ÇAISES | (Paris) Sept. 15/21, 1966 |
| Rapf, M. | LIFE | (New York) Oct. 27, 1967 |
| Riley, G. | LIBERATOR | (New York) Nov. 1967 |
| Rondi, G. L. | IL TEMPO | (Rome) Oct. 27, 1966 |

| Roud, R. | THE GUARDIAN | (London) Aug. 2, 1966 |
| Sacchi, F. | EPOCA | (Milan) Sept. 18, 1966 |
| Sala, A. | IL CORRIERE D'IN-FORMAZIONE | (Milan) Sept. 1, 1966 |
| Sarris, A. | THE VILLAGE VOICE | (New York) Oct. 5, 1967 |
| Scagnetti, A. | PAESE SERA | (Rome) Sept. 1, 1966 |
| Seguin, L. | POSITIF | (Paris) 1966, no. 80, pp. 15–16 |
| Simon, J. | THE NEW LEADER | (New York) Oct. 9, 1967 |
| Solmi, A. | OGGI | (Milan) Sept. 11, 1966 |
| Stringa, E. | CINESTUDIO | (Milan) 1966, no. 18 |
| Thirad, P. L. | POSITIF | (Paris) 1967, no. 86 |
| Toti, G. | VIE NUOVE | (Rome) Sept. 15, 1966 |
| | TIME | (New York) Sept. 29, 1967 |
| Verdone, M. | BIANCO E NERO | (Rome) 1966, nos. 9–10 |
| Winsten, A. | THE NEW YORK POST | Sept. 21, 1967 |
| Yoffe, O. | CINEMA NUOVO | (Milan) 1966, no. 184 |
| Zambetti, S. | CINEFORUM | (Rome) 1966, no. 60, pp. 821–833 |